The Gospel of Mark

New Metaphysical Version

Translator: Bil Holton, Ph.D., LUT

Editor: Cher Holton, Ph.D., LUT

Patricia, your energy, commitment, & love for this ministry are truly gifts of Spirit. Thank you! Bil Holton

Prosperity Publishing House

The Gospel of Mark
New Metaphysical Version
©2008 Prosperity Publishing House
All Rights Reserved

The *New Metaphysical Version* text may be quoted in any form (written, visual, electronic, or audio) up to and inclusive of one hundred twenty five (125) words without the express written permission of the publisher, providing notice of copyright appears on the title or copyright page of the work as follows:

> *The Scriptural quotations contained herein are from the Gospel of Mark, New Metaphysical Version.*
> *Copyright 2008 by Prosperity Publishing House.*
> *Used by permission. All rights reserved.*

When quotations from the NMV (New Metaphysical Version) are used in non-saleable media, such as church bulletins, transparencies, meditation/prayer readings, etc., a copyright notice is not required, but the initials NMV must appear at the end of each quotation.

Quotations and/or reprints in excess of one hundred twenty-five (125) words, as well as other permission requests, including commercial use, must be approved in writing by *The Gospel of Mark, NMV* Permissions Office, Prosperity Publishing House, 1405 Autumn Ridge Drive, Durham, NC 27712.

ISBN: 978-1-893095-51-9

Library of Congress Control Number: 2007932696

Acknowledgments

I gratefully acknowledge the love, generosity, and financial support of the following people and organizations who helped make this New Metaphysical Version possible: Polly Holton; Linda Holton; Rev. Seymour Lafayette; Greg Dixon; Tammy Summers; Ron and Lorie Rosenberg; Rev Nixon; Unity Spiritual Life Center (Durham, NC); Unity Church of Sarasota, Inc. (Sarasota, FL); and ProsperityWorX (Durham, NC).

I also offer thanks to Nancy Eubanks, who assisted in the creation of this New Metaphysical Version of Mark through her tireless typing, enthusiastic support, and personal insights.

Finally, I offer my heartfelt gratitude and love to my wonderful wife and soulmate, Cher, for her faith, support, love, and incredible editing as she stood by me throughout this entire project.

Table of Contents

Acknowledgments .... *iii*
To Students of Truth .... *xi*

Chapter One
Our Quickened Intellect *1*
The Baptizing Power of the Word *2*
The Temptation to Deny Our Christ Potential *2*
Purposefully Retreating Forward *2*
Quickening Four Key Spiritual Powers *3*
Dissipating Our False Beliefs *3*
The Power of Faith *4*
Emancipating Our Subconsciousness *4*
Cleansing Leprous Thoughts *5*

Chapter Two
Moving Beyond Spiritual Subluxation *5*
From Coma Consciousness to Christ Consciousness *6*
A Consideration of Fasting *7*
Observing the Sabbath Daily *7*

Chapter Three
Taking a Sabbatical From Material Appetites *8*
When Discordant Thoughts Appear *9*
Our Twelve Apostolic Powers *10*
Our Beelzebulic Tendencies *10*
The Genealogy of Spirit *11*

Chapter Four
The Parable of the Sower *12*
The Purpose of Parables *12*
Leaving Lamps Under Bushel Baskets *14*
The Parable of the Growing Seeds *14*
The Parable of the Mustard Seed *14*

    The Dynamics of Parables *15*
    Calming Emotional Storms *15*

Chapter Five
    From Gadarene Demonics to Gadarene Harmonics *16*
    A Jairus Moment and a Hem Touched *17*

Chapter Six
    Rejecting Our Christ Qualities *19*
    Our Mission Is to Outgrow Error *20*
    Our John the Baptizer Quality Neutralized *21*
    The Feeding of the Five Thousand *22*
    Walking on Water *24*
    A Gennesaret Experience *25*

Chapter Seven
    Status Quo Without Soul *25*
    A Syrophoenician Perspective *27*
    Curing Deafening Unreceptivity *27*

Chapter Eight
    Satisfying Four Thousand Concerns *28*
    A Dalmanuthaian Dilemma *29*
    Yeasty Thoughts *30*
    Bethsaida Dynamics *30*
    A Mature Faith Is a Prerequisite For Our Christhood *31*
    Resurrecting Our Divine Connection *31*

Chapter Nine
    Transfiguration *33*
    The Coming and Maturing of Our Elijahness *34*
    Transcending Our Error-Proneness *34*
    Re-Causing Our Experience *35*
    The Least of the Greatest and the Greatest of the Least *36*
    Exorcising Error From Our Consciousness *37*
    The Unquenchable Fire *38*

Chapter Ten
Adulterating Our Spirituality 39
All Christ-Centered Ideas Are Blessed 40
Our Materialistic Bents 40
Divine Order Divinely Ordered 42
Human Ambition vs. Spiritual Aspiration 43
Our Bartimaeic Astigmatism Healed 44

Chapter Eleven
Entering That Place of Abiding Peace Within 45
Cursing Sterile States of Mind 46
Our Inevitable Chemicalization 46
Error Withers in Light of Spiritual Understanding 47
A Clueless Ego Remains Clueless 48

Chapter Twelve
The Parable of Our Evolving Consciousness 49
Our Taxing Pharisaical and Herodian Bents 51
Resurrecting the Divine Standard 52
The Two Greatest Avenues Toward Christhood 53
God's Love Reflected As Us 54
The Pitfalls of Our Scribal Nature 55
Spiritual Poverty 55

Chapter Thirteen
The Chemicalization of Our Coma Consciousness 56
Sense Sludge Removed 58
The Senselessness of Sense Appetites 58
The Wattage and Amperage of Spirit 59
A Consciousness of Abundance 60
Our Christhood May Be Closer Than We Think 60

Chapter Fourteen
Plotting a Spiritual Lobotomy 61
An Alabaster Experience 61
Our Misguided Judas Quality 62

Our Christed Cusp of Consciousness 63
The External 'Suppering' of Spirit 64
Our Free-Fall From Grace 64
Our Gethsemane Experience 64
Spiritual Scruples or Spiritual Gumption 66
Spiritual Limbo Spirited Away 67
Denying Our Divinity 69

Chapter Fifteen
Our Carnal Mind Seeks Spiritual Answers to
   Material Questions 70
Messiahing or Rebelling 71
Making a Mockery Out of Ourselves 72
Crossing Out Error and Duality 73
Gaining Immortality 74
The Gateway to Eternal Life 75

Chapter Sixteen
The Restorative Power of the Resurrection Experience 76
The Magdalene Effect 77
When Potential Becomes Actualized 78
Commissioning Our Consciousness for Christhood 78
Ascended Mastery 79

About the Translator 81
Ordering Information 83

To Students of Truth

It is my position that the Bible, which is the story of humankind's evolution in consciousness, lends itself to four different levels of understanding:

1. literal (historical),
2. moral (sentimental),
3. allegorical/esoteric (intellectual), and
4. metaphysical (spiritual/mystical).

Given that perspective, I believe the awesome richness of New Testament Scripture should be genuinely explored in accordance with each level of understanding, with the proviso that the *fruits* of each understanding are consistent with the teachings of Jesus Christ.

It is also my position that those who read or study Scripture only at the surface level (literal and moral) may miss the deeper Truths associated with the teachings. Unfortunately, a sober look at the effect these two levels of understanding have had on human history uncovers their inability to contribute significantly to creating heaven on earth. These two basic understandings of Scripture generally lend themselves to a condemnation of other faith traditions and tend to be quite exclusive and judgmental in their dogmatic religious practice.

An intellectual understanding of Scripture generally tends to remain a cognitive exercise with little movement toward the wisdom of the heart. Such a perspective generally limits its views to the letter of the law and can be judgmental and fairly rigid in its interpretation.

A metaphysical understanding of Scripture takes Bible students into the realms of the spiritual and mystical. My aim is to give Truth students a metaphysical view that stimulates their thinking and appreciation for the deeper meanings of Scripture. This metaphysical treatment is not meant to be the definitive metaphysical version of *The Gospel of Mark*. Hopefully, it will inspire other metaphysicians to add their wisdom and expertise to the growing body of metaphysical literature.

The inspiration for writing this unique version of *The Gospel of Mark* came from extraordinarily varied perspectives and time periods. It is with deep appreciation that this *New Metaphysical Version* (NMV) was able to use insights from the following giants in metaphysical thought: Philo Judaeus, Origen, Pelagius, Zeno, Plato, Augustine, Hypatia, Dionysius, John Scotus Erigene, Meister Eckhart, George Fox, George Wilhem, St. Teresa of Avila, Friedrich Hegel, Ralph Waldo Emerson, Theodore Parker, Mary Baker Eddy, Emma Curtis Hopkins, Nona Brooks, Paul Tillich, Charles Fillmore, Eric Butterworth, Emilie Cady, Teilhard de Chardin, Malinda Cramer, Emmet Fox, John Murray, Ella Wheeler Wilcox, Annie Rix, Thomas Troward, Ernest Wilson, Elizabeth Sand Turner, Warren Felt Evans, Ernest Holmes, Georgiana Tree West, Alice Bailey, Phineas Quimby, Geoffrey Hodson, Helena Blavatsky, Horatio Dresser, Alvin Kuhn, and Dr. Paul Hasselbeck.

The Biblical Versions used as reference material for the NMV in order to obtain the broadest possible band width of interpretation were: *The New Revised Standard Version, The NIV Rainbow Study Bible Version, The Authorized King James Version, George M. Lamsa's Translation from the Aramaic of the Pashitta, The Oxford Annotated Bible RSV, New International Version, the New Testament in Today's English Version, New American Standard*

Bible Version, Contemporary English Version, 21st Century King James Version, Worldwide English New Testament, and the *Wycliffe New Testament.*

This new version is intended for use along-side traditional versions, many of which are listed above. I recommend using it as a study guide for congregational services, as well as for private study, meditation, and daily readings. It is suggested that traditional Gospel versions be used as supplements to this version so that readers can compare traditional interpretations to the metaphysical content of this NMV verse by verse, chapter by chapter. It is my hope that I have provided both wings and landing gears with this metaphysical rendering so that it is both practical and down to earth. I have opted for understandability and clarity instead of loftiness and vagueness.

I believe it has been to the detriment of all Christian history (as evidenced by the last 2,000 years of religious separatism, inquisitions, and wars) that religious leaders almost with one accord have belittled and condemned the importance and significance of a metaphysical perspective. Thankfully a growing number of Truth students and higher consciousness practitioners today are opting for spiritual growth instead of religious myopia, and recognize that religion's failure to cultivate a healthy respect for a metaphysical approach to Scripture has been both unfortunate and costly. It is not an exaggeration to say this hesitation to explore higher Truths has caused a pathological tear in the fabric of Christianity.

It is my sincere hope that you, the reader, will embrace the hidden wisdom contained in this uniquely metaphysical treatment of *The Gospel of Mark*. I believe you will be enriched beyond measure by the depth of its teachings and by the practical nature of its transcendental wisdom.

The Gospel of Mark

New Metaphysical Version

Chapter One

Our Quickened Intellect

1. The beginning of our spiritual unfoldment comes from the recognition that our Christ Self (Higher Self) 2. underwrites all of our prosperity, abundance and higher good through Its very nature (our Isaiah quality). There is a sense of deeper knowing within us that feels the promptings of our Higher Self and seeks to prepare us for our evolving Christhood. 3. It knows we are God individualized at the point of us despite outer appearances. Our chief task is *spiritual orthopedics;* that is, to walk the spiritual path on practical feet. 4. As we grow in our spirituality we move from an intellectual understanding of Truth principles (our John the Baptizer quality) to a Christed perspective. 5. It is from that higher spiritual perspective that we can celebrate our oneness with Spirit by purging error (the baptism process) from our consciousness. 6. Until we mature in our spiritual growth our intellect is undisciplined in its spiritual perspective and blocks its quickening by Spirit. So, we may be a little rough around the *higher consciousness edges,* so to speak, and still tied to the senses (clothed in camel's hair, wearing leather belt). 7. Indeed, as we transform our thinking we will honor that great Presence within us, our I-Am-ness, which is mightier than our sense-burdened human personality. At this point in our spiritual unfoldment we do not thoroughly understand (untie thong on sandals) the transformation our intellect must undergo. 8. Our intellect is only capable of understanding a certain amount of the implications of error thinking. However, the Christ of us, our I-Am-ness, sees only wholeness and provides us with the guidance we need to purge ourselves completely of error.

The Baptizing Power of the Word

[9.] As we mature in our ability to discern Truth from error, our Christ potential (our Jesus quality) permeates our subconsciousness (Galilee) and energizes the receptive intellect (our John the Baptizer quality), melding it with Spirit. [10.] Once we affirm our oneness with the Christ of us (come out of the water), we can rise confidently and expectantly above old error patterns and find the *peace which passes all misunderstanding.* [11.] At this stage of our spiritual unfoldment there comes upon us a heightened sense of our true identity and our eternal connection with Spirit.

The Temptation to Deny Our Christ Potential

[12.] Our conscious desire to attain higher spiritual consciousness is generally accompanied by thoughts from the wilderness of our sense consciousness [13.] which seeks to distract us and *tempt us to deny* (our Satanic bent) our Christ potential.

Purposefully Retreating Forward

[14.] As we retreat forward by quickening our subconscious energies (go to Galilee) as we focus on our spirituality, we will notice an abrupt cessation in the need to intellectualize (John the Baptizer's arrest) our spiritual growth. [15.] This insight will have major implications in taking our subconscious energies (Galilee) to a higher vibration by arresting the limiting effects of our past programming (the time is fulfilled) which we allow to slow our spiritual growth before we discover our true connection (the kingdom of God has come near) with Spirit.

Quickening Four Key Spiritual Powers

16. As we heighten our spiritual intention to honor Divine guidance and instruction we will be uplifted by our faith (our Simon quality) and strength (our Andrew faculty) which are used to *catching* divine ideas. 17. When these higher spiritual qualities are quickened, they fortify other qualities and we will help raise our own spiritual consciousness and the collective consciousness of the planet. 18. Once we make the Christ decision, our entire consciousness moves in the Christ direction. 19. When we do this, our innate wisdom (our James, son of Zebedee quality) and abiding love (our John faculty) sustain us from falling into needless negativity as those qualities repair and replace our old thought patterns. 20. When these spiritual qualities are quickened, there is usually no hesitation on our part to deepen our spirituality.

Dissipating Our False Beliefs

21. As we focus more on our spiritual growth, we begin to turn our attention (come to Capernaum) from materiality to spiritual pursuits (enter the synagogue). 22. When we deepen our connection with Spirit, we will be astounded at the awesome power of our innate divinity. 23. Despite our decision to grow spiritually (enter the synagogue), false beliefs (unclean spirits) may surface from time to time. 24. These recalcitrant beliefs come from an unenlightened ego which recognizes our desire to express our Christ potential (our Jesus of Nazareth quality) and fears Its expression. 25. Our enthroned Christ potential (our Jesus quality) denies what is untrue of us (rebukes the unclean spirit) 26. causing even the most encrusted false beliefs to dissipate. 27. The absoluteness of our Christ nature rattles the earthbound ego which senses a very real threat to its dominion,

28. particularly in respect to Spirit's purifying influence on our subconsiousness (Galilee) which warehouses the thoughts, memories and defense mechanisms we use to keep ourselves attached to the belief in our unworthiness and to the belief in the illusion of our separation from Spirit.

The Power of Faith

29. It is important to realize that when we move out of our prayerful meditative experiences (leave the synagogue) and step into our daily routines, we must do so with a maturing faith and strength of mind (enter the house of Simon and Andres), accompanied by spiritual discernment (our James quality) and love (our John quality) for humankind. 30. The positive, energetic acticity of these four spiritual qualities acting in concert will have a noticeable healing effect on our sense-burdened (feverish) human soul (Simon's mother-in-law). 31. The Christ of us is able to elevate (lift) our mortal accomplishments (hands) by taking the worry and stress (fever) out of our work.

32. In our unenlightened human experience, (represented by evening or sundown), we are usually beset by pssychological and mental illnesses (demons) which are the result of 33. our rather pervasive error-prone human consciousness (the whole city) which has access to, but hesitates to enter the door (exercise faith) leading to our good. 34. We have only to acknowledge our Christ center to be cured of any human ailment (demon) because at the level of Spirit, we are already whole (demons are speechless).

Emancipating Our Subconsciousness

35. It is interesting to note that before we fully grasp the power of our innate divinity (in the

morning when it is still dark) [36.] our overall sense consciousness will not have caught up to our evolving spiritual attunement. [37.] Our higher spiritual qualities will be quickened first [38.] and then our conscious thoughts will feel the effects of our unfoldment. [39.] Then we will sense the changes in the recesses of our subconsciousness (Galilee) where so many of our false beliefs are stored.

Cleansing Leprous Thoughts

[40.] As we turn from false beliefs and impure inclinations (leprous thoughts) which can compromise our spiritual growth [41.] we have an opportunity to strengthen our connection with Spirit. [42.] If our intentions are pure, we can feel the curative effects immediately. [43.] However, we must be careful. [44.] So often our enthusiastic initial steps become mis-steps because there is a certain amount of naiveté and awkwardness that comes with our attempts to tell others about our spiritual progress. [45.] Our premature attempts to retail our newfound spirituality usually result in our deciding to keep a lower profile until we can learn to control our exuberance.

Chapter Two

Moving Beyond Spiritual Subluxation

[1.] Every time we turn our attention (return to Capernaum) to spiritual pursuits we are truly home. [2.] Such moments are generally characterized by a multitude of thoughts which hover in our conscious awareness as we seek to understand our true nature, the Christ of us (the door). [3.] We may find ourselves experiencing periods of spiritual subluxation (paralysis) which seem to test our whole (four men) outlook.

4. Although we may feel immobilized by what we consider to be dire circumstances, we must give ourselves a faithlift and deny the power of outer appearances (remove the roof) by sorting through (dig through) false impressions so we can lay our fears at the foot of Truth. 5. When we demonstrate that kind of faith, we immediately connect with the Christ of us and are able to give up the false for the real. 6. Worldly thoughts (scribes) may question 7. our ability (authority) to discern Truth from error without seeking the intellect's approval. 8. However, our inner guidance system (our Jesus quality) understands the nature of irreverent thoughts. 9. We might ask ourselves if it is easier to deny thoughts that seek to negate our divinity or simply affirm our wholeness and live the lives we are meant to live. 10. Each of us has within us the power (authority) to free ourselves from worldly illusions 11. by affirming resolutely that we are God individualized at the point of us. 12. Whenever we affirm, with conviction, that we are one with Spirit, we raise our consciousness an octave and our entire beingness at a cellular level responds accordingly.

From Coma Consciousness to Christ Consciousness

13. As we live our daily lives (go to the sea) we will have many opportunities to practice Truth principles. 14. For example, our purely human thoughts of acquisition (our Levi quality) and attachments to the dollars and cents of material gains (tax booth) can be overcome when we commit ourselves fully and completely to our spiritual growth. 15. As we continue our spiritual education (dinner) there will be times when we are influenced by sense thoughts and material appetites. 16. These purely human distractions usually spring from a Pharisaical (perfunctory and dogmatic)

perspective which mindlessly questions our spiritual progress and rationalizes our shortcomings. [17.] But if we keep our spiritual antennae (our Jesus quality) tuned in, we will understand that spiritual growth means transforming our sense consciousness (coma consciousness) into Christ Consciousness.

A Consideration of Fasting

[18.] Sometimes our externally-influenced intellect with its dogmatic bents (our Pharisaical influence) plays games with us. It raises questions like: Why aren't you struggling like most people when it comes to abstaining from sense pleasures? [19.] When these thoughts surface, we can simply remind ourselves that there is only one kind of fasting—abstaining from error thoughts which promote the illusion that we are separate from our oneness with Spirit. When our marriage to Spirit is real, fasting from material appetites is unnecessary because we are already operating above sense thoughts. [20.] It is when we forget our relationship with Spirit that we must conscientiously fast from error thoughts, words and actions.

[21.] Trying to force Truth principles (unshrunken cloth) into a closed mind (old garment) is usually too much for old, stale belief systems. Encrusted error is never ready for a Truth triage. [22.] Neither should we attempt to pour Truth principles into bottled-up religious dogma, because the Truth will fall through the cracks of exclusivity, parochialism, and religious intolerance. It is best to share (new wine) Truth with those (fresh skins) who are open and receptive to spiritual growth.

Observing the Sabbath Daily

[23.] At some point we will actualize our Christ potential (the Jesus of us) to the degree that our daily consciousness will operate as if each day is free from temporal thoughts and sense appetites. This freedom from sense appetites is what the Sabbath represents. [24.] Nevertheless, Pharisaical thoughts (narrowly-focused dogmatic perspectives) may surface and we may question our ability to see the spiritual in the material, the extraordinary in the ordinary. [25.] However, we must remember that we are God individualized at the point of us, and we have a natural urge (love) for spiritual fulfillment. [26.] And so, when we act out of our Christ Consciousness (rest from dogmatic tendencies) we are able to digest (eat) higher truths which a partially-awakened intellect (an Abiathar perspective) is unable to do. [27.] The ability to abstain from temporal expediencies and material inclinations is an innate quality within us. We have not been created to be subservient to error. It is through stilling our mind through prayer and meditation that we find the peace and rest (Sabbath) we need to unfold into our Christhood. [28.] It is because of the Indwelling Christ within us that we have access to the peace that passes all misunderstanding.

Chapter Three

Taking a Sabbatical From Material Appetites

[1.] When we turn consciously to spiritual pursuits (enter the synagogue) we become very sensitive to a decline or erosion in good works (withered hand). [2.] In other words, we become human beings being spiritual instead of human doings doing non-spiritual things. [3.] From our Christ perspective (our quickened Jesus quality) we see the real person behind the error. [4.] We recognize that we have the ability to marinate everyday experiences (abstain, rest from error) in the context of any of our life experiences. When we approach life from this perspective, there is no need for dogmatic religious pronouncements (the Pharisees were silent). [5.] Pharisaical thinking has no place in our working theology. Spirit continually urges us to rest (abstain) from debilitating material appetites and extend our energies toward affirming health and wholeness.

[6.] It will come as no surprise, however, that the part of us that clings to parochial religious interests (our Pharisaical inclinations) and remains attached to sense pleasures (our Herodic propensities) will want to censor our spiritual unfoldment which it considers a threat to its existence.

When Discordant Thoughts Appear

[7.] It is important for us to realize that there is more to us than our conscious personality. We have a subconscious dimension (Galilee) [8.] which is filled with our old psychological tapes and thought patterns that follow us wherever we go. [9.] We must constantly be prepared to rise above our sensory appetites (have a boat ready) by keeping our thoughts spiritually-focused. [10.] What is interesting is that when we focus our attention on our spiritual growth (touch the Master), we find that we have many opportunities to raise the quality of our thoughts, words and actions. [11.] Whenever a discordant sense thought (unclean spirit) surfaces, we automatically lift it to its highest spiritual essence. [12.] When discordant thoughts surface, it is best not to resist them, but to let them pass quickly, recognizing they do not have to be part of our consciousness.

Our Twelve Apostolic Powers

[13.] Whenever we focus on spiritual things (go up the mountain) we lift our essential qualities to their highest essence. [14.] And as we call upon all twelve of our key spiritual energies (disciples) we have the wherewithal to restore order to our entire consciousness [15.] including purging ourselves of corrosive, negative tendencies (demons). [16.] The nature of these higher spiritual qualities is a recognition of Universal Substance (our Simon quality) which is demonstrated as faith (Peter quality) in Its availability; [17.] judgment (our James, son of Zebedee quality) and love (our John quality), two ambitious qualities which must evolve into their higher essences—spiritual discernment and selfless love respectively; [18.] strength (our Andrew quality); the power of the spoken word (our Phillip quality); imagination (our Bartholomew quality); the will to align the human self with our Spiritual Self (our Matthew quality); intellectual understanding (our Thomas quality); our sense of order (our James, son of Alphaeus quality) which keeps us in tune with spiritual laws; renunciation (our Thaddeus quality) which is the ability to eliminate (release) false beliefs; zeal (our Simon the Canaanean quality); and [19.] our penchant for conscious movement toward wholeness and completeness (our worldly Judas quality) which, in its underdeveloped emotional state tends to degenerate into sense obsessions which betray our true wholeness.

Our Beelzebulic Tendencies

All of the aforementioned qualities are our Christed qualities (going home). [20.] Our worldly qualities (crowd) cannot understand (eat) our higher nature. [21.] Our personality, with all of its quirks (our family of worldly beliefs and assumptions), is hesitant to embrace spiritual concepts. [22.] If old Beelzebulic (sense-driven) doubts resurface, we must realize they come from a hyper-defensive ego that feels threatened by our spiritual growth. [23.] How can the illusion of our separation from Spirit (our clueless satanic quality) help us rid ourselves of the very illusion it has created to justify its own existence? [24.] If a set of false beliefs (kingdom divided against itself) contradicts itself, how can such a discordant belief system sustain itself? [25.] And if our overall consciousness (house) vacillates between Truth and error (is divided) we will find it difficult to enjoy happy and productive lives. [26.] Fortunately, the same things holds true for a chronic belief in our separation (Satan rising up against himself) from Spirit. It is a false belief which cannot, and will not prevail. [27.] Once we are centered in Spirit, error thoughts cannot trump spiritual thoughts unless we choose to allow the usurpation.

[28.] The slate on most error thoughts can be wiped clean; however, [29.] the denial of our divinity (Holy Spirit) causes us irreparable—and totally unnecessary—pain and suffering. [30.] We are not to identify ourselves with our mortal personalities. We are potential Christs evolving toward our Christhood. We must always remember that Truth.

The Genealogy of Spirit

[31.] When we become confused (brethren standing outside) in regards to our true identity, we may be tempted to remain attached to old life scripts and emotional default patterns that we believe have served us well in the past. [32.] Our sense-oriented ego with its worldly inclinations (crowd) is quick to point out that our defense mechanisms (brethren) have evolved for our own good to protect us. [33.] We must remind ourselves that our human origins come from unmanifest spiritual images, [34.] that there is no real separation between us and others at the level of Spirit. [35.] Grounded in that higher spiritual awareness (surrendering to the will of God), we come to realize that our true genealogy comes from Spirit, which means the Allness of Spirit is in the eachness of us.

Chapter Four

The Parable of the Sower

[1.] It is important that we take our spirituality (our Christ nature) into everyday experience (beside the sea). When we step into the world, we take with us a multitude of sense thoughts, attitudes, beliefs and values. However, we can still remain centered in our spirituality. [2.] We can choose to see the spiritual in every material experience. [3.] For example, spiritually-oriented thoughts and inclinations [4.] can stay thoughts and remain superficial intentions (seeds devoured by birds). [5.] In other cases our lack of interest (rocky ground) or commitment [6.] may rob our ideas of their potential value. [7.] Other spiritual inclinations (seeds) can get caught in intellectual quicksand or choked by dogmatic myopia. [8.] Fortunately, other ideas sown from our higher consciousness are implemented and bring us immeasurable joy, prosperity, and abundance. [9.] Those who are at one with their Christ nature already know this is true.

The Purpose of Parables

[10.] Sometimes it is best to attempt to understand higher spiritual principles through the use of simply-spun stories. [11.] The reason tools like stories, analogies and metaphors are so effective is because they bypass the myopic ego and filter into our higher consciousness. [12.] Stories can be catalysts for the enlightened mind or catacombs for the rationally-oriented intellect. Stories seem to satisfy a suspicious ego, but their higher essence filters into our subconscious, preparing it to give up the false for the true (the process of forgiveness).

[13.] If we fail to understand the hidden wisdom component tucked into analogies and metaphors, we will miss a valuable piece of the message. [14.] The fact of the matter is, we must take responsibility for seeing the higher truths hidden in simple stories. [15.] We must tune into our heir power to see the metaphorical and allegorical relevance hidden in stories ,because there is a self-limiting human side of us (our satanic impulses) which abhors higher, more spiritual interpretations of scripture and resists any notion of a Higher Power. This adversarial side of us (our satanic tendency) seeks to destroy our spiritual unfoldment. [16.] The insights which come to us during trials and tribulations (rocky ground) can be catalysts for our overall growth and well-being. [17.] But we must act on these insights or we will lose their life-affirming potential. [18.] When we conscientiously honor the Truth of who we are despite our being in the world of appearances (seeds sown among thorns), we can choose to be more receptive to the promptings of Spirit. [19.] However, we must be careful because we can allow the centrifugal force of appealing outer appearances to catch us off guard (choke out the word). [20.] The level of prosperity and abundance we enjoy depends on the strength and depth of our belief in Truth principles.

Leaving Lamps Under Bushel Baskets

21. We may ask ourselves, "Should hidden spiritual truths (lamps) intentionally remain hidden or should they be shared (placed on a lampstand)? 22. By their very nature, higher truths exist to teach us, to help us. 23. Those who are receptive to higher truths will grow to understand them. 24. The more we seek to understand spiritual truths, the more spiritual truths will be revealed to us. 25. And the more attuned we are to the nuances of higher truths, the more enriched our lives will be. It must also be asserted that our unreceptivity to eternal truths will cause us to miss many pearls of wisdom and therefore lose many opportunities to deepen our spirituality.

The Parable of the Growing Seeds

26. A higher spiritual perspective (the Domain of the Divine) is like having access to unlimited spiritual ideas and concepts (scattering and growing seeds) 27. which seem to sprout and grow without conscious effort on our part. 28. The whole process takes place as a result of Divine Order: Mind (stalk), Idea (head) and Expression (full grain). 29. And when the expression of a Divine Idea is in tune with God's Will (the grain is ripe), we can rest assured that the outcome (harvest) will be beneficial.

The Parable of the Mustard Seed

30. With what can we compare the Domain of the Divine (the Kingdom of Heaven)? 31. It is like 'mustard seed' thoughts (small, underdeveloped Lilliputian thoughts) sown in our consciousness. 32. The capacity of even a fleeting spiritual thought (birds of the air) to develop into awesome spiritual insights and consciousness-raising concepts (nests) is amazing.

The Dynamics of Parables

[33.] The Jesus of us (our Christ potential) underwrites all of our thoughts, words and actions at each level of our being [34.] so that the process of our unfoldment is a dynamic inner process which unites the eachness of us with the Allness of Spirit.

Calming Emotional Storms

[35.] There are times when our understanding (day) of spiritual truths may be put to the test, when we seek to know deeper truths (cross to the other side). [36.] We must leave the limitations imposed by mortal thoughts (the crowd) behind and stay poised and centered in a positive state of consciousness (boat) by associating with others who practice spiritual principles (the other boats). [37.] When troublesome events occur (a great windstorm) accompanied by tumultuous emotional upheaval (waves swamping the boat) [38.] we must remind ourselves that there is an Abiding Presence within us which only sees wholeness. [39.] Knowing that all is well at the level of Spirit, we need only to affirm "Peace! Be still!" to remind ourselves that outer appearances have no power over us. Knowing this will calm our emotions so we can respond instead of react to situations. [40.] We may question our lack of faith even though we have experienced many demonstrations of prosperity and abundance in the past. [41.] It will soon become obvious that through our Indwelling Christ we can rise above any troublesome event (wind) and calm any emotional storm.

Chapter Five

From Gadarene Demonics to Gadarene Harmonics

[1.] Deep within our subconscious warehouse of thoughts and experiences most of us have pent-up or 'walled in' thoughts and belief systems (Gadarenic tendencies) which we allow to block our good. [2.] If we are not careful, we can lose our positiveness (step out of the boat) and encounter repressed (entombed) thoughts and feelings we thought were buried long ago. [3.] Some of us allow ourselves to be imprisoned by these repressed emotions (live among the tombs) [4.] to the extent that no amount of intellectual safeguards (chains and shackles) can restrain our self-aggrandizing negativity. [5.] People who stay stuck in these debilitating tendencies react to every life experience through Gadarenic filters (stones). [6.] We must remind ourselves that these repressed emotions have no power (bow down) over our true nature. [7.] The pull of taking personal responsibility and becoming more spiritually awakened brings with it the pain of leaving behind old psychological scripts and self-abasement programs that have given us a false sense of security. [8.] The Truth is, at the level of Spirit we are whole. [9.] When we are faced with such demonic and entrenched negativity, we must understand that many of these tendencies come to us through our subconscious connection with the wounds and bruises of the collective consciousness. We want to understand the nature of these maladies so we can label them and use them to define our human plight. Unfortunately, we run the risk of accepting the dis-ease as part of us (not sending it out of the country—My name is Legion, for we are many). [10.] Some people have incredibly ingrained attachments to repressed material and pride themselves in perpetuating their victim status. [11.] Understand this, we can transform even the most gluttonous, slothful, and obstinate forms of our repressed baggage (swine feeding on the hillside) [12.] by denying its power to be any more than it is (enter the swine). [13.] We affirm (He gave them permission) that there is no duality (the herd of two thousand), that our subconscious and conscious selves are one in Spirit and can compliment each other at the human level. Any and all of the repressed baggage that blocks our spiritual growth will implode on itself (rush down a steep bank) and drown in its own negativity (sea water).

[14.] We become aware that our old belief system can be turned upside down. [15.] Our previously demonic (dysfunctional) perspective can be healed (clothed and in the right mind) although we may not believe it at first. [16.] But our own personal experience tells us it is possible. [17.] Because we generally carry so much negative baggage (programming) around in our subconsciousnesses, we may resist the interior changes we are experiencing, and the growth they imply. [18.] As our repressed material surfaces we may seek to deepen our spiritual understanding and expect instant enlightenment. [19.] But the unfoldment toward our Christhood takes time and requires the purification and revitalization of our entire consciousness. [20.] And so we must concentrate on all aspects of our personality (Decapolis) to lift us out of our coma consciousness (chronic error thinking).

A Jairus Moment and a Hem Touched

[21.] Even though we live, move, and have our being from a positive perspective (boat) we will encounter many opportunities to practice Truth principles. [22.] When we devote ourselves to our spiritual practice, we will find that we may have highly intuitive, although decidedly biased, religious views (our Jairus quality) that can be transformed into great spiritual insights if we are open (bow down) to new Truth perspectives. [23.] Even though our intuitive intelligence (Jairus' daughter) may not have been used for a long time (is dying) we must believe that Spirit can revitalize it. [24.] Our past conditioning and socialization (large crowd) may press us for immediate answers.

[25.] No matter how stagnant we have allowed our spiritual qualities to become, [26.] and in spite of the credence we have given to the self-help prescriptions retailed by hordes of motivational gurus (physicians) we find that we are no more enlightened, and in some cases feel worse off. [27.] Despite all of the higher consciousness detours we may have taken, once we center our attention on the Christ of us (our Innate Divinity) [28.] and realize that we can move beyond the illusion of separation (touch the hem of His garment) [29.] we can be made whole. [30.] Immediately aware of our receptivity, the Christ of us invites us to affirm our commitment. [31.] In our evolving spiritual unfoldment (disciples) we may not be aware of the exact moment when we become more spiritual than material. [32.] The potential Christ of us (our Jesus quality) welcomes our spiritual growth. [33.] Unaware of the full implications of our consciousness cross-over, we must simply trust Spirit (fall down before Him). [34.] Our faith will make us whole.

[35.] Even in the midst of a faith-lift, our commitment to our spiritual growth will be tested by an unenlightened ego which believes there is no such thing as spiritual illumination (the daughter is dead). [36.] However, we must remain strong in our faithfulness and believe in the power of Spirit. [37.] The three spiritual qualities which fortify our Truth walk and give it guardrails are faith (our Peter quality), wisdom (our James quality), and love (our John quality). [38.] When we are faced with the commotion of outer appearances [39.] we can simply deny their illusionary power (the child is sleeping) to limit our good. [40.] Our worldly thoughts will ridicule (laugh at) our growing faith, but all we have to do is keep our attention focused on our Christ Center. [41.] None of our Christ potential is ever lost. And no matter how dead we think we are spiritually, all we have to do is allow ourselves to be guided by Spirit (a talitha experience). [42.] When we demonstrate this level of faith we can experience immediate health and wholeness in all areas (twelve years) of our body, mind and soul. [43.] This is a highly personal process of unfoldment. No one else can unfold our Christhood for us. We must seek to understand (eat) what is ours to understand.

Chapter Six

Rejecting Our Christ Qualities

[1.] Although our body is our biological address, our spiritual home is our Christ Consciousness. [2.] As we abstain from error thoughts (experiencing the Sabbath) our enlightened perspective has a positive affect on our previously dogmatic religious perspective (synagogue). We may ask ourselves where our newfound spiritual insights come from and how we are able to manifest the good we are experiencing with such power and poise. [3.] Our unenlightened ego questions our authenticity because it identifies solely with our human genealogy and feels threatened by our connection to Something it can't comprehend. [4.] The prophet within us (our power to discern and avoid error) is not honored by the materially-focused ego (the hometown of sense thoughts). [5.] Because of the ego's hold on our worldly thoughts (sense thoughts) we are only able to influence (lay hands on) a small number of sense-oriented thoughts (a few sick people) at a time. [6.] It is amazing how unaware of its higher functioning the materially-minded ego is.

Our Mission Is to Outgrow Error

Our life is our teaching and our teachings are our life. [7.] We must call on all twelve of our key spiritual qualities and keep our human ambitions in harmony with our spiritual aspirations so that we can control and eliminate discordant thoughts and inclinations. [8.] It is not wise to be complacent or neglectful in spiritual matters, and we must not burden ourselves with unnecessary attachments to material things. [9.] It would be much wiser to use our ability to discern both the human and divine nature of things (wear sandals). And we must not think we have to over-protect (wear two tunics) ourselves from every conceivable error impulse that surfaces. We are Christed beings. The only extra protection we need is a mind centered on the teachings and example of the Christ. [10.] As we apply our growing awareness of Truth principles to our existing belief system, we must give ourselves time to integrate the learning. [11.] Even if we are not quite ready to release certain beliefs, we don't have to get caught up in forcing ourselves to abandon all of our non-productive beliefs at once. [12.] Clarity will come later, so long as we don't allow lingering sense perceptions to cloud our understanding and compromise our progress. [13.] In this way, we can outgrow (cast out) dysfunctional worldly thoughts (demons) and demonstrate our love (anoint with oil) for our evolving consciousness of Truth.

Our John the Baptizer Quality Neutralized

[14.] At some point in our spiritual unfoldment our materialistic ego becomes acutely aware of the inevitable influence our Jesus quality (our Christ potential) has on our evolving intellect (our John the Baptizer quality) which has a tendency to renew its on-again-off-again interest in comprehending spiritual truths. [15.] Our paranoid ego may even believe it is being tormented by an external presence of unfettered power (Elijah) or simply by an old dogmatic belief system (prophet) that it has cultivated to protect itself. [16.] But the sense-oriented ego generally concludes that most of its troubles come from a reform-prone and inquisitive intellect which must be discouraged (beheaded) in its efforts to seek a higher level of spiritual functioning.

[17.] As ruler of our human personality, the ego (our Herodic tendency) is fully aware that it can keep the intellect in check by tempting it with sense gratifications (our Herodias influence) which distract it (hem it in) from its intellectual pursuit of the concept of right-ness. [18.] In its effort to promote right doing, the intellect sometimes runs afoul of an ego obsessed with sense pleasures. [19.] Our sense gratifications (our Herodias influence) usually seek to neutralize (kill) the intellect's troublesome quality, which takes the form of a 'do-good conscience.' But our need for gratification is subject to the ego's influence and always follows the ego's lead. [20.] Although the paranoid ego would love to dismiss the inquiring nature of a characteristically rigid intellect, it respects the intellect's capacity for discernment, which has helped protect the ego's rulership many times.

[21.] The sense-prone ego's recurrent predictability (birthday) stems from its repressed urges which are warehoused in our subconsciousness (Galilee). ²². When purely carnal urges surface (our Solome, daughter of Herodias inclinations), they seek wholeness (dance) like any other subconscious urge which excites the intoxicated ego. ²³· The excited ego, eager to experience the heights of physical ecstasy, is usually willing to sacrifice its intellectual inclinations (half its kingdom) in order to enjoy the pleasures of the flesh. ²⁴· In our unbridled search for new sensual fulfillments (our Solome influence), we depend on the lessons we learned from past sensual experiences (our Herodias influence) to justify not paying attention to our conscience (ask for head of John the Baptizer). ²⁵· Assured of the rightness of choosing the sensual over the intellectual ²⁶· we prepare to plunge, libido first, into the throes of carnality. ²⁷· Our sense-prone ego rationalizes (sends a soldier) the necessity of neutralizing (beheading) the reform-conscious intellect (our John the Baptizer quality) ²⁸· and straight-away cuts the intellect's reticence out of the equation (head on a platter). ²⁹· When we fail to bridle our sense temptations, our higher spiritual values (disciples) are still able to sustain us (take the body) and prepare us for future demonstrations of abstinence over carnal desires (lay body in tomb) and give us the strength for the entrainment necessary to become one with our Christ nature.

The Feeding of the Five Thousand

³⁰· To walk the spiritual path on practical feet we must focus our thoughts on our Christ Center. ³¹· It is the place of spiritual wholeness that we can find the rest we need to distance ourselves from material thoughts. ³². Oftentimes, as we enter the silence (go away in a boat) ³³· many worldly concerns may surface and interrupt our prayers

and meditations. ³⁴· We may even choose to come out of our meditative experience (go ashore) so we can put Truth principles into action, particularly when it comes to transforming mortal thoughts (sheep without a shepherd) into their higher spiritual equivalences. ³⁵· At the human level we may feel bound by circumstances that appear to offer us nothing but lack and limitation ³⁶· and so we may settle for sensory fulfillment instead of spiritual sustenance. ³⁷· But Spirit knows we are blessed with ever-present Substance, even though we mistakenly see lack and limitation because we still believe in duality (buying two hundred denarii worth of bread. ³⁸· If our only discernment is through our five senses, we will identify with lack, or fail to appreciate the resources we have. ³⁹· When we trust in the abiding Presence of Spirit we will feel grounded (sit on the grass) in Truth. ⁴⁰· This groundedness affects our whole being (hundreds of people) and vivifies our five senses (groups of fifty people). ⁴¹· When we believe in the eternal now-ness of Universal Substance (five loaves and two fish), bless our abundance, act on faith (break the loaves), and use our spiritual gifts (disciples) to serve others, we will essentially eliminate the belief in duality (divide the two fish and feed all). ⁴²· And when we truly understand (eat) who we really are, our human personality will become one with our Spiritual Individuality (we will be filled). ⁴³· At this level of consciousness each of our twelve spiritual powers (twelve baskets) will be quickened with an endless supply of Universal Substance. ⁴⁴· And it is from this exalted perspective that all five of our natural senses will evolve toward their higher spiritual essence.

Walking on Water

[45.] We must constantly rise above our sensory appetites (get into the boat) and focus on a consciousness of abundance (Bethsaida). [46.] Although we have earthly obligations and responsibilities, we must keep them in perspective (say farewell) when it comes to our spiritual growth (go to the mountain to pray). [47.] Once we are able to put our worldly concerns aside, we can enter that state of consciousness where we become consciously one with Spirit. [48.] What is interesting to note is that when we depend only on our human abilities (strain at the oars against an adverse wind), we tend to get tossed around a bit by life's experiences, feeling rudderless and exposed. However, Spirit's Omnipresence is always available, ready to guide us and sustain us. It sees only wholeness (passes them by). [49.] Sometimes we find ourselves in such an emotional upheaval that we're not sure the guidance we're receiving is from Spirit or of our own making (ghost). [50.] But Spirit speaks to us in that unmistakable still small voice that says, "Relax! Take a deep breath. You are not alone. I am here. Do not give power to outer appearances." [51.] When we allow the Presence of God to express Itself as us, the emotional surges (winds) of doubt and fear will subside and cease to knock us off course. The results will be so compelling [52.] that we may miss the full impact of the ever-present nature of Eternal Supply (the loaves) and neglect to trust (harden our hearts) in the unfailing availability of Divine Substance.

A Gennesaret Experience

[53.] From a sense of oneness with Spirit, we sense a unity with all of life (a Gennesaret experience) [54.] and find that our spiritual predisposition produces positive thoughts and attitudes as we go about our daily living (step out of the boat). [55.] Even when thoughts of separation and doubts about our spiritual worth surface, [56.] including fairly ingrained beliefs and concepts (villages, cities and farms) which keep us focused on the mundane aspects of life, we can find the peace, health and wholeness we need by taking the first step (touching the fringe of the coat) toward the practical application of Truth principles.

Chapter Seven

Status Quo Without Soul

[1.] Occasionally we allow ourselves to fall from a place of peace (Jerusalem) into hypocritical religious perspectives [2.] and question the direction of our spiritual growth, especially the manner in which we modify existing religious practices (eat with defiled hands) to suit our spiritual growth. [3.] It is important for us to understand (eat) that dogmatic and traditional religious thinking are usually unreceptive (wash off) to the beneficial effects we can gain from a metaphysical perspective. [4.] Such a closed belief system is satisfied with only a literal interpretation of scripture. As a matter of fact, when we limit our spiritual perspective to purely religious parochialism, we miss the truths that we can gain from other faith traditions (cups, pots, kettles). [5.] Dogmatic religious perspectives will not help us appreciate the richness of higher spiritual truths. [6.] What an unfortunate mistake. Our Higher Self, the Christ of us, holds us to a higher spiritual standard. When we give lip service to Spirit without true surrender to Spirit [7.] our counterfeit discipleship is in vain, because hiding behind dogmatic and judgmental religious doctrines perpetuates the belief in separation from Spirit, and compartmentalizes people instead of uniting people under the common bond of love. [8.] When we graft ourselves onto these narrow views we abandon movement toward our Christ Individuality and settle for the limitations inherent in our human personality.

[9.] We have become quite good at deluding ourselves when it comes to spiritual matters. [10.] We may believe in turning negatives into positives (our Moses quality) and intend to honor traditional religious ordinances (father) and practices (mother). We may even feel led to defend deeply ingrained religious viewpoints. [11.] But the underlying motive is hypocrisy [12.] since there is no real intention to honor the spiritual tone of religious values. [13.] Under those circumstances, we practice hollow religion instead of hallowed spirituality.

[14.] We need to understand the relationship between our thoughts, actions, and reactions. [15.] It is not what is said or even done to us that defiles us but what comes out of us that shows the level of our spiritual maturity and the quality of our consciousness. [16.] We must understand this important truth if we are to objectify our spirituality.

[17.] When we move from (enter the house) worldly thoughts (crowd), our spiritual perspective (disciples) can be strengthened. [18.] Our growing faith in the triumph of Truth over error will help us understand the dynamics of true spiritual discernment. [19.] Much like our stomach on the physical level digests healthy as well as unhealthy food, our consciousness has the ability to absorb Truth and dispose of error. [20.] It is the thoughts, words and actions that spring from us that show others how spiritually mature or immature we are. [21.] An error-prone disposition comes from a mortal consciousness embedded in sense delights that can lead to a host of ills [22.] which seem to produce a lifestyle characterized by missteps. [23.] Any thought or intention which negates our oneness with Spirit contaminates our consciousness. Our fall is an inside job.

A Syrophoenician Perspective

[24.] We are sensory beings (our Tyrean receptivity) in our outer expression, and spiritual beings at our core. So our higher thoughts cannot help but be noticed [25.] by our intuitive intelligence (our Syrophoenician quality) [26.] which senses our higher spiritual nature and seeks to help us move past our worldly thoughts (our Gentile inclinations) so that our innate love for the Truth (daughter) can express itself rightly. [27.] All potential Christed thoughts must be nurtured (fed) so that no expression of Truth is lost. [28.] Even a fleeting thought based on Truth enriches those instinctive aspects of our lower nature (dogs) that are hungry for a glimmer of enlightenment. [29.] The Christ of us rewards this kind of intentionality [30.] and can turn even a fleeting inclination toward repentance into a spontaneous life-changing event.

Curing Deafening Unreceptivity

[31.] We must consciously be aware of our human tendency to get caught up in sensory distractions (our Tyrean influence) and the ideas which are produced by them (our Sidonic proclivities), and withdraw our attention from worldly inclinations by concentrating on our interior spiritual wholeness (Decapolis), so that even our subconsciousness (Galilee) is positively affected. [32.] It is here we must recognize that within us which is unreceptive (deaf) and resists expressing (speech impediment) the Truth. [33.] The best thing we can do is go deeply into the Silence (privacy away from crowd) so that we can completely block out all unnecessary mental chatter (divine spittle). That will allow us the wherewithal to express the Truth (touched deaf mute's tongue). [34.] In that state of higher consciousness we will find ourselves totally open and receptive—mind, body and soul (an epiphanian moment) to Divine Guidance. [35.] Our receptivity will be fully apertured (ears opened) and our ability to express Truth blessed with incredible discernment (tongue released). [36.] This level of divine receptivity is far above the threshold of awareness (tell no one) of our egocentric consciousness. However, the more spiritualized aspects of our mortal consciousness sense there is something very special going on and are energetically aroused (zealously proclaim it). [37.] These spiritually sensitive parts of us realize there is more to us than mere flesh and blood awareness.

Chapter Eight

Satisfying Four Thousand Concerns

[1.] As we continue our Truth walks, we will notice that the more we know, the more we realize we don't know. [2.] We will reach spiritual plateaus where we feel little to no evolution in our body, mind, and soul's connection to Spirit. [3.] There is always a concern about our ability to actualize our Christhood, [4.] and we may question from time-to-time if we can manifest (feed people) our good in the midst of perceived lack and limitation (desert). [5.] If we turn to the Christ within (our I-Am-ness) we will recognize our wholeness at the level of Spirit, and our ability to manifest what we need through the creative process (seven loaves of bread, which represent the seven-step process of manifestation: initial awareness, confirmation, imagination, will power, wisdom, love and stillness). [6.] All we have to do is quiet our multitude of concerns by grounding ourselves in principle, declaring the omnipresence of Substance, expecting to be blessed with divine ideas and guidance, and then giving thanks for our good, believing in the spiritual Truth which affirms as above, so below. [7.] It is important for us to bless even the seemingly insignificant divine ideas (a few small fish) we have. [8.] When we put Truth principles into practice, we will experience many avenues of health, happiness and abundance. And we can manifest each of those ideas using the same seven-step creative process mentioned in verse five. [9.] All of our mental faculties, the fullness of our intellect, our intuitive abilities, and even our childlike qualities will be vitalized. [10.] We must not take the ability to manifest our good for granted, especially in the early stages of our spiritual growth when our capacity to understand our spiritual connection tends to get stuck in dogmatic judgmentalness and self-serving hypocrisy (our Dalmanuthaian dilemma).

A Dalmanuthaian Dilemma

[11.] Our ego's Pharisaical and materialistic nature demands external proofs of our emerging Christhood. [12.] Unfortunately, we can become incapacitated by the limited perspectives generated by dogma, judgmentalness, and hypocrisy and fail to see our innate divinity and the innate divinity in others. [13.] If we find ourselves in such a Dalmanuthaian dilemma, it is best to change our perspective by thinking positively (get into boat) so that we can focus our attention on our divine purpose.

Yeasty Thoughts

[14.] Sometimes we forget about the spiritual us, and the material us takes over. When that happens we may forget all about ever-present Substance. [15.] Our Christ nature cautions us to beware of Pharisaical thoughts and putting our egocentric will (our Herod quality) ahead of Divine Will. [16.] We may ask ourselves why our belief in Omnipresent Supply has slipped our mind. [17.] We may even be surprised we still have thoughts of lack and limitation. We may ask ourselves if we have forgotten that God is Absolute Good, everywhere present. [18.] We have the ability to understand spiritual truths, yet fail to use it. We have the capacity to hear higher truths, yet remain unreceptive. Do we remember that we are God individualized at the point of us? [19.] Do we forget how many of our thoughts we have raised to a higher spiritual vibration; [20.] and how many of our subsequent thoughts and inclinations have also been elevated to a higher spiritual octave? [21.] What will it take for us to put aside yeasty thoughts based on outer appearances, and faithfully embrace the Truth that the ever-present availability of Divine Substance is just an affirmation, a positive thought, a prayer, a faith-lift away?

Bethsaida Dynamics

[22.] Even though we may have an over-all consciousness of prosperity and abundance (Bethsaida) there may be lingering beliefs of lack and limitation (blindness) that block our good. [23.] When this happens it is best for us to change our direction by seeking the clarity of Spirit (saliva on eyes) so we can do what we've come to do (laying-on of hands). We must do this expectantly. [24.] We must move beyond the plethora of intellectual concepts (trees) [25.] and trust Spirit to help us gain the spiritual restoration and enriched vision we need to move from the head to the heart. ²⁶·It is important that we ground ourselves in Truth principles (go home) before we attempt to make wholesale changes in our overall lifestyle (village).

A Mature Faith Is a Prerequisite For Our Christhood

²⁷·Oftentimes when our domineering conscious personality (Caesarea Philippe) becomes aware of Spirit, we struggle to understand the nuances between Truth and error. ²⁸·Our first instincts are to try to grasp our true nature through the intellect (our John the Baptizer quality), or our religious over-zealousness (our over-enthusiastic Elijah quality), or other intellectual means. ²⁹·But it takes more than the intellect's mechanics to discern spiritual truths. It takes mature faith (our Peter quality) to understand who we really are. ³⁰·As mentioned in the previous passage, the same caution holds true—we must understand that we must move from our head to the heart before we can quicken all twelve of our spiritual qualities. Only through that disciplined receptivity to our quickening can we fully manifest our Christhood.

Resurrecting Our Divine Connection

³¹·There is that within us (our Jesus quality) which knows that our trips through egocentric territory to get to our spiritual centers can involve great suffering, particularly as we attempt to release old programs and patterns of beliefs. These encrusted ego-driven tapes and personality hang-ups can kill our spiritual inclinations unless we take an active role in Divinely Order-

ing our experience. [32.] Unless we have a fully-developed faith, we may think Divine Order is something outside our sphere of influence. We may believe Divine Order is something that happens to us instead of from us. The Truth is we divinely order our experience. The quality of that experience depends on our ability to express Christed ideas instead of egocentric ideas. [33.] On again-off-again faith can become a stumbling block in our spiritual development because its focus tends to be influenced by our belief in the illusionary power of outer appearances (our Satanic tendency) instead of the resurrecting power of Spirit. It must be emphasized that we divinely order our experiences through our Spirit-led expression of Divine Ideas.

[34.] We must understand that the total constellation of our thought universe, our sense thoughts (crowd) and our spiritual thoughts (disciples), must deny the rulership of the personality through the process of spiritual discernment so that we can cross all error out of our lives. [35.] When we remain tied to sense consciousness, we will miss the joy of an enriched spiritual beingness, and when we opt out of an error-riddled life by choosing to follow Truth principles, we will find the inner peace, joy and enduring comfort we seek. [36.] For what will it profit us to live our whole lives based on the belief in our separation from Spirit? [37.] Indeed, what will we have to show for a life centered solely on material appetites? [38.] If we purposefully neglect our spiritual growth by cultivating a consciousness of material aggrandizement (adulterous and sinful generation) we will lose our ability to discern the difference between Truth and error (our innate Son of Man super-quality).

Chapter Nine

1. Truly, when we understand the Truth and are not led astray by error thinking (taste death) we will feel the powerful effects of living, moving and having our being in our Christ Consciousness.

Transfiguration

2. It is through the Christ as us that our faith, wisdom, and love are lifted up to their highest spiritual essences. When that happens we are literally transfigured by the flow of divine power throughout our entire being. 3. We experience an electrifying change in consciousness that radiates our physical appearance. 4. It naturally follows that the Truth of our I-Am-ness rises from the depths of our subconscious with unobstructed and unfettered power. 5. So vivified, our ability to manifest our Christ nature (punctuated by our Jesus quality) so we can rise above negation (our Moses quality), and our ability to demonstrate the awesome power of our I-Am-ness (our Elijah quality) become strong inner promptings. 6. As a result of such powerfully expressed Christed inclinations our Christ potential (our Jesus quality) experiences energetic vibrations which have hitherto been dormant (speechless). 7. While we are experiencing this fantastic transcendentalness, we are overcome by a state of cosmic bliss which envelops us so that we experience what it's like to fully connect with the Beloved Son (the Christ Principle) within us. 8. Because we are not quite ready to assume full Christhood, our Christhood is still more potential than conscious expression at this point in our spiritual unfoldment.

The Coming and Maturing of Our Elijahness

9. When we come down off our spiritual high, we realize we cannot share such a transformative experience with those who have not experienced a similar transcendental rush. 10. Even though we may have experienced it first-hand ourselves, we may still question our capacity to fully restore our I-Am-ness. 11. There is a part of us, our over-exuberant, but purely human nature (the under-developed Elijah quality within us) which may find it difficult to release the concept of an external deity. 12. We must realize that our overly-enthusiastic inclination to focus on an external God characterizes our initial spiritual growth. Many people are under the impression that an anthropomorphic God in the sky watches over us and will come again to take us home. 13. As we deepen our spiritual understanding we will come to realize that the omnipresence of Spirit is individualized in us, through us, and as us. When we make that distinction, we realize that our I-Am-ness has always been at the core of our being.

Transcending Our Error-Proneness

14. As we grow in our overall spiritual awareness (our quickening disciple qualities) nescient, worldly thoughts (the crowd) come to us, including old, myopic religious views (scribes), which indicate how much more we need to learn. 15. However, we have an overall sense (crowd) that we are on our way to awesome personal growth and discovery. 16. We may wonder why we wander from the Truth. 17. Despite this insight we find ourselves having high spiritual inclinations one moment and purely materialistic impulses the next which seem to negate our

progress (inability to speak). [18.] This vacillation immobilizes us and affects our ability to clearly articulate (foam at mouth and grind teeth) spiritual truths. Habitual vacillation between Truth and error is a self-defeating process. [19.] Such an on-again-off-again Truth walk is a perverse walk. It is a Jekyll and Hyde theology which must be out-grown and purged out of our consciousness.

[20.] The good news is, error loses its footing in the face of Truth, [21] no matter how engrained or entrenched error may be. [22.] Our attempts to purify our thinking (cast into the fire) and move beyond our negativity (water) will continue to be difficult unless we grow spiritually. [23.] When we recognize our Christ potential (the Jesus of us) we can move beyond any perceived limitation. [24.] With a little soul searching we can identify the cause (father) of our current difficulty (the effect or child) and see wholeness instead of lack.

[25.] Such a faith-lift can reap huge dividends and enable us to move beyond any apparent difficulty. [26.] Sometimes it may take some good old-fashioned 'kicking and screaming' to rid ourselves of fits of error-thinking so that discordant thoughts lose their power (become corpses) over us. [27.] When this happens, our Christ potential (our Jesus quality) puts us back on solid spiritual footing. [28.] We cannot eliminate error thinking merely because we have a basic knowledge of spiritual truths and feel we are tapping into our spiritual powers (disciples). [29.] Erasing error requires a disciplined habit of going into the Silence (prayer/meditation).

Re-Causing Our Experience

[30.] Quite often, it seems, the changes that take place in our subconscious (Galilee) are subtle. [31.] We must remind ourselves, however, that an undisciplined and suspicious ego, ruler of our human personality, will be persistent in its desire to stunt our spiritual growth and kill Divine Ideas. However, all we have to do is re-cause our experience by divinely ordering our ideas (three days signifies the three-step process of divinely ordered experience—Mind, Idea, Expression) which lead to divinely ordered choices which produce divinely expressed actions. [32.] That means every choice we make can be a Christ choice, and every action we take can be Christ-centered.

The Least of the Greatest and the Greatest of the Least

[33.] The more we devote ourselves to live a Truth-principled life, the greater will be our yearning to lift others and ourselves out of error consciousness. This enduring compassionate state of consciousness (Capernaum) helps us distance ourselves from competing material thoughts (arguing along the way) which vie for our attention as we sort out Truth from error. [34.] We may ask ourselves which of our thoughts and divine ideas is the greatest thought or divine idea. [35.] This reasoning is purely natural as we ponder our spiritual growth. However, it is important that we not prematurely judge thoughts and divine ideas which come to us. The ideation process works this way: Initial ideas become the foundation for later ideas which become the foundation for still newer ideas which become the foundation ... you get the point. So which is greater, the initial idea or its offspring? The same reasoning applies to our innate spiritual qualities. Which quality is greater, an old mature one or a newly-developed one? [36.] It is important to know the significance of improving an existing spiritual quality, developing a new one, or wrapping our minds around a new idea (little child). [37.] When we grasp the essence of the nature of divine ideas, and particularly new insights, we will understand the concept of the least of the greatest and the greatest of the least. Whenever we welcome a Divine Idea from the awareness that it comes from Spirit, we welcome the Christ as us into our lives.

Exorcising Error From Our Consciousness

38. As we tighten our love connection (our John quality) with the Christ of us, we become very aware of our secular as well as spiritual thoughts and inclinations. It may seem odd to us that at some point our purely human instincts become increasingly sensitive to our growing spirituality and uncharacteristically censor error thoughts (cast out demons) without consciously realizing where the impulse comes from. When this happens we tend to second-guess ourselves and question our motive. 39. But exorcising error from our consciousness is Christed work, whether it comes from our higher spiritual awareness or our mortal awareness. When our mortal consciousness becomes more sensitized to Truth, it is an indication that our human personality is deepening its entrainment with Spirit. As that entrainment evolves, our human personality will lose its focus on separation (the erroneous belief that we are not one with Spirit) and out-grow its denial (speak evil) of our innate divinity. 40. Any thought, whether it is based on spiritual principles or secular intentions, which produces Christed results is a demonstration of our spiritual unfoldment. 41. Every thought, inclination, choice, or action expressed knowingly or unknowingly from our core being, which is the movement of the Christ as us, will be blessed.

The Unquenchable Fire

42. Any time we disregard or intentionally censor Divine Ideas and their creative expression, we are creating stumbling blocks which weight us down in the burdensome negativity of error consciousness. 43. If we are tempted to see discordant actions as normal or settle for error-prone handiworks, we must break those patterns and censor the thoughts which cause them, or 44. we will remain in a permanent state of separation from Spirit (unquenchable fire). 45. And if our understanding (foot) is such that we perpetuate the illusion of our separation from Spirit, 46. we will remain in eternal ignorance of our divine nature (hell). 47. If all that we perceive is based on a consciousness of separation, it is better for us to at least make an attempt to perceive spiritual reality (the realm of the divine) than live our whole lives in a state of chronic error (hell) 48. which produces pathological tendencies (worm that never dies) that consume us, fictionalizing our worth, and keeping us in a perpetual state of Truthlessness.

49. All of us have within us the innate ability (salt) to understand our true nature so that we can attune ourselves with the Universal Spiritual Energy that burns off the dross of our materially-oriented sense consciousness (being salted with fire). 50. Although we come pre-wired, so to speak, with the ability (salt) to comprehend our divine nature (God individualized at the point of us) we must use that ability to season our spirituality. This Truth cannot be emphasized enough. We must develop the ability within ourselves to see ourselves as individualized expressions of God and help others to see their divine connection so there can be peace in every corner of the world.

Chapter Ten

Adulterating Our Spirituality

1. When we consciously move beyond the limitations posed by error thinking, we become more Christlike in our expression and quicken the energies in our subconscious mind so that our inner light shines. This allows us to transform all of our thoughts from error to Truth, and therefore, raise the octave of our overall consciousness.

2. Even though we reach this level of spiritual development, we can be tested by Pharisaical thoughts (dogmatic thoughts). For example, we may ask ourselves, "Should I keep my feeling nature separate from my thinking nature?" 3. In order to gain that understanding we must be able to draw upon the Truth within us. 4. It usually takes that kind of introspection, because error thoughts generally rule in the darkness (our ignorance of the Truth) and can surface as we seek to better understand ourselves. 5. It will occur to us that we may still be naively fundamental in some of our religious beliefs that see separation instead of unity in body, mind, and spirit. 6. Unity is the Truth of us because our thinking and feeling natures are the chief components of our consciousness. 7. For this reason, our thinking nature can outgrow its previous conditioning and fully complement our feeling nature, 8. uniting with it and entraining with it toward our higher, more spiritual essence. 9. We must understand with absolute certainty that there is no separation between our thinking and feeling components and our Christ nature, which takes these two components to their highest spiritual essence, which is wholeness and oneness with Spirit.

10. As we elevate our thinking (enter the house), our higher spiritual qualities (disciples) are energized and our ability to

grasp the union of thoughts and feelings is heightened. [11.] It becomes perfectly clear that whenever we exchange one error thought or belief for another error thought or belief we are, in fact, adulterating our spirituality; [12.] and if we allow a highly charged feeling to trump (divorce) sound reasoning so that it engenders another feeling that perpetuates the myth of separation, we adulterate our spirituality all the more.

All Christ-Centered Ideas Are Blessed

[13.] Everyday we receive ideas (children) which we believe have spiritual origins. Until we reach a certain level of spiritual maturity we may question an idea's origin. [14.] But the Christ of us encourages us to welcome, unconditionally and joyfully, all new spiritually-oriented ideas, no matter how fleeting; for that is the chief requisite for entering the Kingdom of God (Christ Consciousness). [15.] If we fail to express our Christ potential (come as a child) it will be impossible for us to fulfill our Christhood. [16.] Rest assured Spirit will bless all of our Christed thoughts.

Our Materialistic Bents

[17.] Inevitably, a Christ-inclined, but personality-encumbered thought surfaces and with it the desire for unlimited prosperity. [18.] Deep down we know the proper course of action we must take to achieve the wholeness and peace of mind we seek. And we know the Source of that abundance. [19.] We also intuitively know the necessary Truth principles to practice: We must not kill divine ideas or spiritual impulses; we must choose spiritual thoughts over carnal ones; we must not think we can walk the spiritual path with material feet; we must refrain from telling partial truths to satisfy materialistic desires; we must not claim to be something we are not. We must honor the thoughts and feelings which come from our Christ Center. [20.] We may tell ourselves we already do those things. But we may still harbor a sense of incompleteness. [21.] And here's the reason: We know that in order to be perfect expressions of our Christ Nature we must give up the need for all worldly attachments and the temptations which foster them, so that we do not place them ahead of choosing our oneness with the Christ of us. [22.] Until this fully sinks in, most of us pay more attention to material appetites than to living Christ-centered lives.

[23.] However, there is that within us, our Jesus quality (the Christed us which has mastered thinking and living above material thoughts and appetites) which recognizes our human dilemma. [24.] Although we are aware of our growth in key spiritual areas (disciples) we may still consider movement toward our Christhood a daunting task. While we may not fully understand our evolving Christ potential (our childlike awareness) we must clearly understand that our Christedness is predicated on its potential being actualized. [25.] The Truth is, it is easier for a camel to go through the eye of a needle than for our material-minded human personality to still itself long enough to achieve Christ consciousness. [26.] In consideration of that last statement we may ask ourselves, "Who can possibly attain Christhood?" [27.] But the Jesus of us, which has attained Christ status, is our Way Shower and knows that when we operate out of our mortal (coma) consciousness we see nothing but separation from Spirit and thus delay our Christhood?"

[28.] If we truly have faith in the reality of our oneness with Spirit we will be able to leave all material attachments behind so that we possess our possessions instead of our possessions possessing us. [29.] When we leave stale, self-defeating, error-prone beliefs and materialistic urges behind and seek our oneness with Spirit, [30.] we will receive the fantastic enlightenment which comes with the higher level of consciousness (in this age) which we have achieved. Our old, dated life scripts and error patterns which we allowed to cause our suffering will give way to the constancy of our Christed life. [31.] We will gain an extraordinarily expansive spiritual consciousness. And each thought that comes to us matures rapidly and takes our thought universe to a higher octave, so that each thought becomes the foundation for the thoughts which follow. The cumulative result is a leap in consciousness nourished by the constant influx of Christed thoughts.

Divine Order Divinely Ordered

[32.] When we center our awareness on that place of abiding peace within us (Jerusalem), our entire beingness (disciples) will feel that power of our Christed vibration. [33.] In this exalted state of spiritual bliss, our ability to discern Truth from error will be tested by an unenlightened ego bent on suppressing our spiritual urges while promoting our material appetites (hand over to the Gentiles). [34.] If we are not careful, we may sacrifice (mock) our spiritual inclinations by opting for material delights. However, if we remain steadfast on our Truth walks, we can divinely order our experience (represented by the three-day time period) by turning our worldly impulses into Spirit-filled expressions of peace, health and wholeness.

Human Ambition vs. Spiritual Aspiration

35. There may be times when our personal ambition seeks to turn our wisdom and love qualities into their lower vibrations: judgmentalness and desire for material gain. 36. While the Christ of us is always open to our expanded awareness, It is able to discern material impulses from spiritual aspirations. 37. So, as we seek to deepen our spiritual understanding, and refine our wisdom and love qualities in particular, we may think we can cultivate both human ambitions and spiritual aspirations equally because we are still attached to the belief in duality (sitting at the right and left hand). 38. If that is where we are in consciousness, we truly don't understand the nature of our journey toward Christhood. The question becomes obvious: Do we think we can attain eternal life (drink from the cup) without cleansing our mind (a baptism in consciousness) of all materialistic attachments and desires? 39. We will obtain eternal life once we have cleansed our consciousness of all material appetites and attachments; 40. but, to think we can cling to our belief in duality and achieve an enlightened consciousness is purely ours to work though.

41. It should be clear that love and wisdom, or any of our spiritual qualities for that matter, which are lowered to their unquickened state can temporarily upset our spiritual cart. 42. Worldly thoughts (Gentiles) unchecked and unmonitored, can handcuff our spiritual progress. 43. But we must choose to allow our egotistical ambition to give way to healthy spiritual aspirations, 44. and the spiritual qualities we wish to define our growth must have service to all as the primary guiding principle.

45. Discerning Truth from error produces within us a desire to serve, not to be served. Every time we formulate a

Truth thought, it cancels out an error thought. In that sense, Truth thoughts are the ransom we pay for purging our consciousness of unhealthy worldly ambitions, attachments, and illusions.

Our Bartimaeic Astigmatism Healed

[46.] When we refrain from intellectualizing our spirituality (leave Jericho behind), that part of us which is blinded by old, established beliefs and life scripts (our Bartimaeus penchant) [47.] finds itself groping for answers that a frightened and confused ego is powerless to provide. We have a sense that spiritual understanding can only come from our heart center (our David quality) and yet our encrusted attachment to old, stale life patterns prevents us from the clarity we seek. Nevertheless, we see the need to decontaminate our consciousness, hoping to gain the insights we need to edit and perhaps even rewrite our old scripts. [48.] It will come as no surprise that the journey from the head to the heart can be a difficult one, and our error-riddled ego will object strongly to our groping toward the light. But we must persevere. [49.] Our Christ potential (our Jesus quality) is ever ready to remind us of our wholeness and calls us to faithfully move toward the Christ light within us. [50.] We can start by relinquishing our attachment (toss off the cloak) to the false impressions inherent in outer appearances and look within. [51.] By looking within through prayer and meditation (going into the Silence) we can hear the still small voice that comes from being in the Presence of our I-Am-ness. In that stillness we need to say, "Holy Spirit, let me remember that I am God individualized at the point of me." [52.] When we demonstrate that level of faith and awareness in our connection with Spirit, we will live a Christed life.

Chapter Eleven

Entering That Place of Abiding Peace Within

[1.] When we go to Headquarters, that place of inner peace within us (Jerusalem), we reach a state of grace (Mount of Olives) characterized by a high degree of love and wisdom. [2.] From that state of grace we can move beyond our worldly ambitions and the consciousness (village) which produces them, and demonstrate a newfound willingness (colt which has never been ridden) to surrender to the promptings of spirit. [3.] Instead of trying to second-guess ourselves, we must remind ourselves that these qualities can be elevated to their highest spiritual vibrations. [4.] Because we are willing to surrender to the Christ within (door), we are showing that we have complete trust (untying the colt) in Spirit. [5.] If we should have any doubts (by-standers) of our worthiness [6.] all we have to do is remind ourselves of our innate Christ potential (our Jesus quality) and affirm our readiness to fulfill our spiritual purpose. [7.] We can prove our mastery over base human desires by recognizing and honoring our Christ potential (Jesus sits on colt). [8.] This surrender to Spirit shows our resolve to release our worldly attachments (cloaks) and use our collective resources (palms) to do what we have come to do. [9.] When we find ourselves in that state of grace we won't be able to contain our joyfulness (hosannas) because we will recognize the incredible spiritual potential we possess. [10.] And knowing what we know, we will enthusiastically expect the advent of universal love (the coming of the Kingdom of David) as the over-all spiritual consciousness of the world is elevated. [11.] When we stay centered in that place of abiding peace within us (Jerusalem), we can deepen our experience (go into the temple) by being vigilant of the nuances associated with our interior growth (look around at everything), and use that spiritual maturity (lateness of the hour) to move beyond any and all sorrows and afflictions (Bethany), especially since all of our highest spiritual qualities (twelve disciples) have been quickened at this stage of our spiritual unfoldment.

Cursing Sterile States of Mind

12. As we demonstrate our ability to move beyond human limitations (Bethany), we hunger for the spiritual truths these experiences hold for us. 13. In our quest for Truth and the anticipated enlightenment (figs) it brings, we expect to uncover hidden truths in everyday experience, and we are disappointed when we don't find them. For example, when we come across a literal interpretation of scripture (a fig tree in leaf only) we know that it will produce little, if any, spiritual richness beyond its face value. Its lack of depth (barrenness) presents only a myopic view of the endless possibilities of spiritual insights of which it is capable. This is regrettably unfortunate. 14. Without the light of a more Christed understanding the chances of gleaning, and thus appreciating, the deeper truths inherent in all scripture are almost non-existent to the closed mind. Our higher, more quickened, spiritual faculties (disciples) position us for comprehending spiritual truths, but we must develop and apply those energetic faculties.

Our Inevitable Chemicalization

15. As these energetic faculties are quickened and we spend more time abiding in that interior place of peace

(Jerusalem) called the Silence, there begins to occur a depth charge of inner transformation that intensifies and leads to what can be a rather volatile process of cleansing and purification. The fusion of enlightened thought and stale belief systems causes an internal combustion which sends specks and flecks of our ego's insecurities and hang-ups to the surface. Our materialistic tendencies are uprooted (tables overturned) and our worldly resistance to spiritual nonresistance (doves) acquires a new perspective (overturned seats of money changers). This tumultuous growth process is called chemicalization and the interior transformation that occurs is demonstrable and enduring. [16.] The chemicalization process ensures that toxic thoughts and bleaching beliefs which have contaminated our consciousness are forced out of our body (temple) and therefore unable to inflict further damage. The therapeutic benefits of this cleansing process cannot be over-emphasized. [17.] Our consciousness is the epicenter of communion with our Christ Nature and must not in any way, shape or form, become a repository for retailing and perpetuating errors. [18.] Our narcissistic ego is extremely uncomfortable with the meltdown of material tendencies. And it is particularly concerned about the inclemency of Spirit in ridding the body of error. [19.] The good news is we can overcome the unenlightened ego's discomfort with our spiritual transformation and rest in the peace that passes all misunderstanding.

Error Withers in Light of Spiritual Understanding

[20.] With increased spiritual understanding we will be conscious of the effects of a diminutive dogmatic perspective (withered fig tree) which bleaches scripture of its true value. [21.] Our vigilant faithfulness (our Peter quality) in applying Truth principles will help us recognize debilitating dogma when we see it. [22.] Our faith in the unerring guidance of Spirit will sustain us. [23.] As the Jesus of us (our Christ potential) unfolds, we will not only be able to discern hidden truths quickly, we will be able to rise above any human limitation, no matter how negative or foreboding it may seem. The Truth is error withers in light of spiritual understanding. [24.] When we live at the speed of our Christ Consciousness, whatever we affirm from our Christedness will unfold according to the pattern of wholeness that it truly is, which is the will of God.

[25.] When we affirm our direct and indivisible connection with Spirit through conscious communion (prayer), we give up our fixation with fiction. That sensory fixation is our attachment to anything which limits or blocks our spiritual growth. Giving up our fixation with fiction is the process of forgiveness, which is at its true essence emotional amnesty. This is an important practice because the Immutable Principle of Eternal Being (the Father) is the Restorative Agent which underwrites the whole process of cleansing error from our consciousness. [26.] If we fail to give up our fixation with fiction, we lengthen (trespass against) the restorative process, and thus prolong the journey to our Christhood.

A Clueless Ego Remains Clueless

[27.] When we get really good at our Truth walks and are able to stay connected to Spirit in such a way that we are constantly in a state of peace (Jerusalem), the effects that level of consciousness has on our physical bodies (temple) on an emotional and cellular level is amazing. Every part of our makeup feels the increased liveliness and energetic flow of Spirit (walking in the temple).

Our biased and error-prone predispositions (chief priests, scribes and elders) also sense the higher vibratory distillations of Spirit. ²⁸·Because we are influenced by these ruling predispositions, we may question the Source of our liveliness and increased vitality. ²⁹·But Spirit knows our materialistic predispositions must evolve into spiritual perspectives, otherwise the understanding it takes to recognize the Source of our eternal vibrancy is moot. ³⁰·We may ask ourselves, "Is it possible for our intellect to deny the power of outer appearances when it has no knowledge of Universal Substance or of the Omnipresent nature of Spirit? ³¹·We must stop second-guessing our spiritual instincts. ³²·Otherwise we will dampen the intellect's inquisitive nature, which senses there is more to life than the materialistic bents of an unenlightened and confused ego. ³³·Without comprehending Divine Guidance, the unenlightened ego is truly clueless as to where the Source of our spiritual good originates. It remains tethered to the same illusions it spins to perpetuate its pathological belief in duality. Therefore, it cannot possibly lift us out of the illusions it purposefully manufactures.

Chapter Twelve

The Parable of Our Evolving Consciousness

¹·This analogy takes us to the heart of why we find ourselves in this particular earth experience. Within us is the Kingdom of Heaven (vineyard) which is the domain of the divine. This heavenly domain is implanted in our consciousness and surrounded by our physical body (the fence around it). Our vital energies (wine) are pressed by our earthly experi-

ence (the pit) in the process we call evolving toward our Christhood (watchtower). God's Presence is literally morphed into us as us so we can have immediate and sustained access to Spirit. And God's Presence operates at the level of omnipotence (the far country), a level of consciousness to which we aspire as we deepen our Truth walk. [2.] We have passport-free access into the Kingdom because Divine Mind (the vineyard owner) has given us the awareness (our mental servant) to collect our impressions (divine ideas) and express them in ways that create services and products (produce) for the good of all that come from a spiritually-oriented consciousness (vineyard). [3.] If we choose not to enter the Kingdom (Realm of the Divine) or refuse to accept the guidance of Spirit (send Him away empty-handed), we limit our earthly good (our Adamic inclinations) and slow our spiritual progress. [4.] To make matters worse, in our initial attempts at spiritual growth, we may disregard our divine origin (insult the Source of our good) and attempt to rationalize (beat over the head) our human destiny in some other way. [5.] But Spirit's love for us is eternal and so we are equipped with that innate urge which seeks to do right. It is an intellectual perception (our John the Baptizer quality) that is not quite quickened at this stage of our evolving Christedness. Our sense inclinations are so strong and pronounced that we may opt for sense pleasures and trump (kill) our sense of rightness. [6.] Fortunately, we have within us the Christ Standard (Beloved Son) that is God's Presence and Perfection grafted spiritually onto us. [7.] Unfortunately, knowing intellectually that we are God individualized at the point of us and that the Christ of us (our Heir power) is an integral part of us, we may still miss the point of our divine potential and deny (kill) our oneness with Spirit. [8.] When we deny (kill) our oneness with Spirit we live a life filled with illusion (throw Him out of the vineyard). [9.] We might ask ourselves how such thinking will benefit us. There is a deeper, more Eternal Part of us that knows the answer. This cannot be made more clear: We will not fulfill our Christhood, in this incarnation or the next, until we move beyond the illusion of our separation from Spirit and declare our oneness with the Christ of us.

[10.] The process described above is the evolution in human consciousness. It is the story of our on-again-off-again relationship with Spirit. The Incarnated Truth (the Stone) that has been rejected for centuries is the Indwelling Christ Principle (the Cornerstone) [11.] of God's Grace (the Lord's doing). [12.] Our unspiritualized ego is a product of its own fantasies and will do everything it can to perpetuate its illusions. It wants to arrest any thoughts or inclinations which fail to support its paranoia. Although it fears and distrusts the inquisitive qualities of the intellect which can generate many interesting and worrisome ideas (the crowd), it still believes the intellect is bound by the belief in outer appearances (coma consciousness) and, therefore, can be controlled. Without a sense of divine connection (they left him and went away) we tend to retreat from our divinity, missing the opportunity to identify ourselves with that Eternal Part of us, our Christ Self.

Our Taxing Pharisaical and Herodian Bents

[13.] Sometimes Pharisaical and Herodian thoughts surface which seek to undermine our evolving spirituality. [14.] These thoughts, Pharisaical (our dogmatic, literally-focused tendencies) and Herodian (our encrusted religious beliefs that attempt to manipulate and misrepresent spiritual truths) come to us disguised as sincere desires to understand the Truth. We may feel justified giving into worldly appetites, but still expect spiritual growth. [15.] Unfortunately that rationale will get us nowhere because the Christ of us, aware of the hypocritical nature of sense thoughts sees into the heart of the matter [16.] and exposes the rationalizations for what they are. [17.] Hopefully we can come to our senses and realize that material thoughts produce material outcomes and spiritual thoughts bring spiritual outcomes. Once this clarity is achieved, we are able to put our dogmatic and manipulative religious bents aside.

Resurrecting the Divine Standard

[18.] From a purely materialistic standpoint (our Sadduceean perspective), some of us find it difficult to believe that we can truly elevate our thinking from sense consciousness (coma consciousness) to Christ Consciousness. This error belief is engrained in our collective consciousness because we have allowed our egocentric intellect to dance around the concept of Absolute Truth. [19.] However, it is important for us to value sense thoughts for their potential spiritual worth. [20.] The manifestation process (moving something from thought to form, from invisible to visible) involves seven steps or phases, and the whole process is the result of the marriage between our human personality and our Christ Self.* If one phase fails to build the momentum it needs to move an idea toward manifestation, the creative idea will not a move to its next stage of unfoldment (childlessness). [21.] If the same thing happens in each phase of the creative process [22.] there

---

The process of transforming thought into things is a seven-step process: initial awareness, insight, imagination, resolve, wisdom, love, and stillness.

will be no creative result at all. And if we lose our desire (the woman dies) to put creative thoughts into action, we will not manifest the things we need to fulfill our purpose. [23.] But once a new thought surfaces, we need to repeat each phase of the "idea to manifestation" process in order to forge the material out of the immaterial.

[24.] However, we must not doubt the creative power of Spirit, because whenever we connect with the Christ of us we automatically receive Divine Ideas. [25.] Every time we raise ourselves to the Christ Standard of thinking, our ideas are Divine Ideas and do not need to be melded (married) with Spirit because they are already Divinely Ordered (angels in Heaven). [26.] And, as for the ideas we never implement, we need only remember God's promise to us: We will always have the power to reproduce an unlimited supply of ideas [27.] because the creative process is built on new ideas and not spent concepts. Those who do not believe in resurrection (the realization that we can be restored to the Divine Standard) have much to learn.

The Two Greatest Avenues Toward Christhood

[28.] When we have a worldly disposition we tend to have worldly thoughts (our scribe nature). And from that materialistic consciousness we tend to miss the whole point of our earthly existence, and wonder how we can organize our thinking and experiences in such a way that our lives work for us. [29.] When we endeavor to follow the inner promptings of Spirit (our Israel consciousness) and strive to deepen our spirituality [30.] we will know without a doubt that the best way to deepen our connection to Spirit is to resolve to completely integrate the wisdom of the heart and the higher intellect with our soul essence at all levels of our being. And that means allowing the Allness of God, individualized as us, to work in, as and through us so we can express our Christedness.

³¹· And the second most important spiritual practice is to see the divine potential in all the thoughts springing from our human personality (our neighbor) as well as the unbroken spiritual connection of every living thing. This realization will help us see that the Christ is the Real Self of all of us, because we all come from the same omniscient, omnipotent, omnipresent Source. There are no other guiding principles as important as these two injunctions. ³²· If, in our worldliness (our scribe nature), we can truly bring these realizations into conscious awareness by declaring the presence of the Indwelling Christ in our body, mind, soul, ³³· and to honor the Christ potential in our human personality (our neighbor), and all living things as aspects of ourselves—this understanding is much more important than all of the rhetoric (burnt offerings) and positive things we do and say (sacrifices) to offset the error thoughts we have. ³⁴· If this is truly our understanding, we will have taken an important step toward our Christhood (the Kingdom of God).

God's Love Reflected As Us

³⁵· We can remain dogmatically immovable (our scribe orientation) and stay attached to a literal interpretation of scripture, which limits our understanding of its deeper meaning, or strive for a higher understanding of scripture. For example, how can divine love individualized in human consciousness (our Davidic quality) be greater than the Christ of us (our Messianic quality) which gives it expression? ³⁶· It is that very quality of divine love in us and as us which keeps us in daily communion with Spirit. As long as we remain focused on the Christ as

us, our thoughts, words and actions will be Truth-oriented, and eventually, our enemies (our Pharisaical tendencies) will give way to a deeper and more abiding understanding of the Truth. ³⁷· God's love is reflected as us because It is individualized in us and is a spiritual anointing which gives us the wherewithal to harmonize any and all egocentric discords (large crowd) and transform them into their higher spiritual essences.

The Pitfalls of Our Scribal Nature

³⁸· As we mature in our spiritual orthopedics, walk a disciplined Truth walk, we come to an awareness that we must be very conscious of the noise level of our worldly inclinations (our scribal nature) which artfully conceal our going through the motions (wear long robes) while we pretend to show interest in spiritual matters. ³⁹· We must also be careful of inbred religious dogmas (synagogues) and traditional intellectual theories (banquets) of what it means to be enlightened. ⁴⁰· When we are in this sense-oriented frame of reference, we allow our worldly belief systems (widow's houses) which come from the human half of our over-all consciousness to consume (devour) all of our thoughts, words and actions. We may even pretend to commune (pray) with God for appearance's sake. Unfortunately, we will reap what we sow.

Spiritual Poverty

⁴¹· The Christ of us stands ready to provide the guidance we need to grow into our Christhood from Its higher vibration within us (sits opposite the treasury which represents our religious but outer appearance-prone consciousness). Many of our thoughts, rich in materiality, are evidence of our

spending most of our thoughts (large sums of money) on material pursuits. [42.] Even though most of us tend to put our spirituality on hold and operate out of a worldly perspective (widowhood) most of the time, there are times when we devote all of our thinking and feeling nature (two small copper coins) to a spiritual pursuit. [43.] It may not seem like much, but our spiritually-oriented thought (one penny, or mite) is worth more than many materialistically-oriented ones. [44.] Most of us have little difficulty generating worldly thoughts; but, when we are able to step beyond a consciousness of lack (spiritual poverty) long enough to see spiritual possibilities, we can leave our old worldly consciousness behind (all that we had to live on), on our quest to understand our relationship with Spirit. Even a brief spiritual moment is worth more than an abundance of worldly moments which stunt our spiritual growth.

Chapter Thirteen

The Chemicalization of Our Coma Consciousness

[1.] Whenever we come out of a good meditation experience (come out of the temple) we become especially sensitive to generally accepted worldly concepts (large stones) and prevailing belief systems (large buildings) which are built on the illusionary power of outer appearances. [2.] When we are in touch with the Jesus of us (our Christ potential) we will be able to see through the superficiality of rudderless belief systems built on the shifting sands of sense consciousness, and realize that false concepts (stones) built on false concepts cannot prevail.

[3.] When we have reached an exalted state of awareness (a Mount of Olives consciousness) characterized by a total commitment to Spirit, we will notice that spiritual qualities such as faith, wisdom, love and strength of mind will be energetically raised to their highest essences. ⁴· We will be tempted to look for confirmation, and even validation (signs) of our spiritual growth outside of us. ⁵· However, we must remember that we are Christs in the making (our Jesus perspective) and monitor our thoughts so that we can discern the false from the True. ⁶· Many of our thoughts and inclinations will come from that fractured part of us, our warped and materialistic ego, which believes in separation. Giving in to those kinds of thoughts will lead us to stray from the awareness of who we really are. ⁷· Because our worldly-bound ego is so attached to the illusions it spins, we will go through what has been called the dark night of the soul (wars) and a period of emotional upheaval and mental questioning (rumors of wars). Some refer to this cleansing of our consciousness as chemicalization. However we choose to label it, it is a process we all go through as we prepare to leave our worldly consciousness behind (the end is still to come) and continue to reclaim our true nature on the way to our Christhood.

⁸· Our spiritual unfoldment requires that each of our ruling worldly thoughts (nation) will question (rise against) its higher spiritual counterpart (nature), and each sense-manufactured belief system (kingdom) will compete with its exalted spiritual counterpart (nation). Belief systems will be rocked from their foundations (earthquakes) and there will be a lack of confidence and faith (famines) in existing secular structures and perspectives to provide the answers we feel we need to manage our lives. The good news is, this is but the beginning of our birth pangs (the initial chemicalization phase) of our deepening spiritual unfoldment.

Sense Sludge Removed

⁹· Be under no illusion. Those who seek their Christhood will undergo an entrainment process (graduated spiritual alignment) which has what many will consider to be a formidable adversary in the form of a frightened and extremely paranoid ego with its divisive assumptions (governors and kings). It will be prepared to torture and kill any evolving divine idea it considers a threat to its existence. ¹⁰· And, yet, we must hold fast to the Truth that we are individualized expressions of God as us (the good news) and affirm that all of our worldly concepts (nations) have the potential to become Christed thoughts. ¹¹· When we allow our ego to justify its perspective (bring us to trial) by tempting us to follow our sense-deluded appetites (hand us over), we must stand firm and realize that we can divinely order our experiences (whatever is given to us to say) because it is from this level of awareness that the Holy Spirit speaks as us. ¹²· Sibling thoughts will seek to censor (kill) opposing views; engrained, established beliefs (fathers) will refuse to accept (kill) new perspectives and the potential (children) they bring. ¹³· We may even choose to remain in our limited sense perspective (coma consciousness) in spite of its form-centered lawlessness and spiritual void. However, when we remain steadfast in our inner development, we will cleanse ourselves of the sense sludge which we have allowed to keep us stuck in error.

The Senselessness of Sense Appetites

¹⁴· When we sense the dissolution of our material consciousness taking place, it is evidence of our evolving spiritual judgment and cause for much jubilation (our Judean faculty) as we center ourselves in our higher

beingness (flee to the mountains). ¹⁵·Once we are operating at a higher spiritual frequency (on the housetop) we will have little to no attachment to lower states of consciousness and the error-proneness which takes up residence there. ¹⁶·Nor will we want to give up limitless growth to wrap ourselves up in limitations associated with sense perspectives we've outgrown. ¹⁷·Those who remain pregnant with old concepts or settle for nursing stagnant sense thoughts will find their advance slowed or even halted. ¹⁸·We must pray that as we soar toward higher octaves of spiritual consciousness, we remember that the process involves going from a sort of spiritual hibernation to a perfect state of our divine unfoldment. ¹⁹·It is at this stage of our spiritual unfoldment that we will fully appreciate our struggle toward Christhood. ²⁰·We will realize that if we had not chosen to cut ourselves off from (deny the power of) material appetites, we would not have regained conscious awareness of our innate divinity. ²¹·Because of our disciplined spiritual growth we will be able to separate the false from the true. ²²·We must constantly be on guard because our unenlightened ego prides itself in its ability to deceive us, to lead us astray, no matter how advanced we think we are on our spiritual walk. ²³·Eternal vigilance is the key. We have all we need within us to fortify us and to sustain us.

The Wattage and Amperage of Spirit

²⁴·When we choose error (the sun darkened) over Truth, our unenlightened intellect (the moon failing to radiate its light) ²⁵·will lose its ability to shine (stars fall from heaven) and our ability to produce divine ideas will be compromised (the powers of heaven shaken). ²⁶·However, when we reaffirm our ability to discern

Truth from error (see the Son of Man coming in clouds) our worldly thoughts will lose their vitality and influence over us. ²⁷·In this state of renewed awareness we can receive energetic Divine Guidance which bathes our entire consciousness with the wattage and amperage of Spirit.

A Consciousness of Abundance

²⁸·We must remember this about Divine Substance: The more aware we become of its omnipresence, the more able we are to manifest abundance. ²⁹·And each time we manifest abundance, we are reminded how well Truth principles work. ³⁰·Clearly, we need to live, move and have our being in higher consciousness in order to demonstrate consistent abundance. ³¹·Divine ideas and their manifestations will come and go, but rest assured that the Consciousness which underwrites them is Eternal.

Our Christhood May Be Closer Than We Think

³²·It is important to be faithful on our Truth walks because we do not know the moment when we will actualize our Christhood on earth. Absolute Good can sense that vibration. ³³·So, we must faithfully practice Truth principles so we will be ready. ³⁴·Our Christ Actualization can be moments away. For example, it can happen when we come out of a prayer/meditation experience (leave home) and know that we are prepared to apply our spiritual knowledge (put servants in charge) in whatever circumstance we find ourselves. We must honor the immediate access we have to our Christ potential (doorkeeper) by taking every opportunity we can to turn our Christ potential into our Christ Presence. ³⁵·It cannot be over-emphasized—we must

be eternally vigilant in all stages of our earthly sojourn. ³⁶· If we are not prepared we may miss (sleep through) our Christ Moment. ³⁷· We must not doubt for one moment, one nanosecond, that Christhood is available for every one of us. We must practice the Principles (stay awake, watch).

Chapter Fourteen

Plotting a Spiritual Lobotomy

¹· Although intellectually we may still have a sense of duality (two days), we also sense we are moving toward a cusp in consciousness, which means we are going into an advanced state of awareness characterized by an errorless state within our body, mind and soul (unleavened bread). However, our worldly and religiously dogmatic nature (chief priests and scribes) conspire to arrest the notion of our Christ potential (the Jesus of us). ²· Even though the paranoid ego, using the intellect's hard, cold logic, would like to perform a spiritual lobotomy, it is hesitant to confront the spiritual part of us it doesn't feel equipped to understand, let alone decipher the nuances between error and Truth.

An Alabaster Experience

³· Because of our Christ potential (our Jesus quality), we are able to overcome leprous inclinations which can corrupt the health of our vital energies. Our selfless love and devotion to unfolding our Christ Nature and our willingness to offer Spirit our best (an alabaster experience) characterize our spiritual growth. ⁴· However, there are still purely human parts of us (prone to anger) which ques-

tion what they consider to be our lavish devotion to Spirit. [5.] We may believe, for example, that it is okay to use our heightened spiritual powers for purely material gain. Unfortunately, the same process (mind, idea, expression) used to manifest divinely ordered ideas at its highest essence is also the same process that can be used to manifest selfish and materialistic ideas from a worldly perspective. Sometimes, it seems, our *getting mentality* scolds our giving inclinations and finds ways to justify our selfish motives. [6.] But the Jesus of us (our Christ potential) is well aware of our evolving spirituality, and in particular any affirmative acknowledgement of our growth. [7.] Although we tend to live in our sense consciousness, and have worldly thoughts (the poor) fairly regularly, we do not normally live, move, and have our being at our highest spiritual essence until we are more spiritually advanced. [8.] Our disciplined devotion to fulfilling our Christhood invites us to bury our selfish instincts forever. [9.] Clearly, whenever we consciously and consistently demonstrate our devotion to Spirit, our entire consciousness (the whole world) is revitalized, even at a cellular level (will be held in remembrance).

Our Misguided Judas Quality

[10.] No matter how "spiritual" we think we are, there is that within us (our covetous Judas quality) that is intellectually committed to our higher spiritual purpose, but clings to a belief in lack, and uses that self-deluded vulnerability to justify material pursuits at the expense of our spiritual growth. [11.] If we fail to transform our covetousness (the unquickened, lower quality of our Judas faculty) into its higher, more spiritual phase (philanthropy), we will steal vital energy from our spiritual growth.

Our Christed Cusp of Consciousness

[12.] When our spiritual growth evolves to the point that we are on the brink of attaining Christhood, our heightened consciousness will produce a telling energetic effect on perfecting our body, mind, and soul (unleavened bread). We may wonder how best to prepare ourselves for such a transformation. [13.] Initially, we must take a balanced spiritual approach (two disciples) into our daily living (city) and discover that we can manage (carry a jar) our emotions (water). [14.] There is no need to doubt our ability to maintain our composure because the Christ of us knows when the "turning point" which heralds our Christship will take place. [15.] It is important to remember that at the level of Spirit (large room upstairs, furnished and ready) we are already Christed beings. [16.] So, our chief task in life is to prepare ourselves for our greater good by keeping ourselves Christ-centered each-consecutive-moment-of-now.

[17.] As we near the completion of our current cusp of consciousness, we will notice how evolved our higher spiritual qualities (disciples) have become. [18.] And while we attempt to understand (eat) our newly-acquired state of consciousness, we may sense an element of betrayal [19.] because there is a part of us that is still attached to materiality, particularly since we have allowed most of our previous thinking to be ruled by a materialistic ego. [20.] The Christ of us is aware that we are spiritual beings in human form (dipping bread) and human beings spiritually formed (the bowl called human experience). [21.] Through our Christed Self, we are able to discern the difference between Truth and error. We are entirely responsible—and accountable—for our thoughts, words, choices and actions. If we choose error (betrayal) over Truth our spiritual void will be greater because our fall from grace will be greater.

The External 'Suppering' of Spirit

22. When we internalize (eat) the full implications of the Omnipresence of Divine Substance (bread) we will transcend any and all beliefs in limitation. 23. And when we have risen completely above the attachments of an unenlightened ego (drink from cup) 24. we will experience an incredible 'transfusion of consciousness' (blood of the covenant poured out) whereby we receive a purer strain of Divine Consciousness. 25. When we achieve that level of sanctification, our Christhood is assured.

Our Free-Fall From Grace

26. As illumined beings in the making (the singing of the hymn) our lives will become symphonies of wisdom, love and joy (a Mount of Olives experience). 27. When we reach this level of illumination, our adeptship may be severely tested by a stunned and shunned ego. 28. Even when we have reached this spiritual pinnacle 29. we may not realize how our faith will be called into question. 30. As incredible as it may seem, we may still have the tendency to sink into diddlysquat order* (deny me three times) instead of Divinely Ordering our experience in accordance with spiritual principles. 31. Oftentimes, it is with the best of intentions that we promise Spirit that we will remain faithful to our spiritual growth. Although we refuse to believe we can fall from grace, especially since we know how much we have grown spiritually, we will stumble unless we remain Christ-centered.

Our Gethsemane Experience

32. Despite our commitment to realizing our Christhood, we

---

*Failing to divinely order Spirit-anointed experiences

must undergo the agonizing process of completely letting go of our attachments to the negative aspects of human consciousness (the Gethsemane experience). [33.] We will need all of the faith, love and wisdom we can muster because it will be difficult to detach ourselves from the sense attachments of human beingness. [34.] We will actually go through a grief process because our worldly attachments are so strong. [35.] We go to Gethsemane every time we agonize over having to deal with our human attachments which we know present barriers to our spiritual growth. [36.] These attachments are the "cup which must pass from us" as we seek to align our will with Spirit's.

[37.] When we purposefully descend into our subconsciousness to purify and cleanse that aspect of our human-ness which warehouses all of our human experience, our faith may waiver because we remember the intense struggles we have experienced in order to transform our old, stale belief systems and patterns of living. It is natural that we want to avoid re-experiencing (are caught sleeping) the pain associated with that part of our spiritual growth. [38.] When we are connected to the Christ of us, we will recognize our dilemma and prepare ourselves to face our perceived vulnerabilities head-on (the spirit is willing, but the flesh is weak). Our initial descent is to make sure our mind is attuned completely with Divine Mind.

[39.] A second descent is necessary so that we can assure ourselves that all of our ideas will be Divine Ideas, exact representations of the Will of God. [40.] We must realize we will resist (sleep through) this phase of examining our ability to divinely order our experiences. It, too, is emotionally, intellectually, and physically exhausting (our eyes are heavy) because we remember the difficulty in ascertaining if our ideas were actually Divine Ideas.

⁴¹·Our third descent helps us examine the quality of our expression of Divine Substance so that its manifestation is Divinely Expressed. As mentioned before, we generally resist (sleep through) this descent because we realize the awesome responsibility of divinely ordering (manifesting) the perfect Will of God as we purge our subconsciousness of negative influences and tendencies. The process of perceiving the difference between Divine Order and diddlysquat order tests our readiness for Christhood. We will want to ensure that we have extracted all covetousness (inclinations toward betraying our commitment to our Christship) from our consciousness. ⁴²·Although our intentions are good, our sense-oriented faults must be overcome (the betrayer is at hand).

Spiritual Scruples or Spiritual Gumption

⁴³·Even as we near the realization of our Christhood, there is that within us (our covetous and worldly Judas quality) which resists relinquishing our attachments to materiality, and so we attempt to justify our sense-orientation through counterfeit beliefs and philosophies (the large crowd of priests, scribes and elders). ⁴⁴·And one of those philosophies is to refuse to release our material attachments and ambitions by having no scruples in choosing to betray (Judas kiss) our intimate relationship with our Christ Self in order to satisfy material appetites. ⁴⁵·Even against our better judgment we unhesitatingly betray our Christ potential when our personal ambitions trump our spiritual aspirations. And the unsettling thing about it is we know what we are doing (he said to him, "Rabbi"). ⁴⁶·Once we have set our selfish inten-

tions in motion, Spirit allows our trespass because it has given us the power of choice. [47.] Our misplaced faith in our ability to manage both material and spiritual pursuits simultaneously may cause us to feel that we can use the self-righteousness of our cause (sword) to limit the influence (cut off the ear) of our worldly consciousness, particularly as it relates to opposing spiritual views. [48.] Because we have the power of choice we can decide to betray our spiritual growth at any time during our unfoldment. [49.] The Christ of us is constantly guiding us and teaching us through the still small voice of Spirit, and out of our receptivity to hear divine promptings, we can choose to follow our Christedness or continue our worldly attachments. But we must move beyond worldly enticements, even if it means going through dark night of the soul experiences (purifying all of the aspects of our sense consciousness) which test our commitment toward unfolding our Christhood. [50.] So great may be our trials that our spiritual gumption may fail (desert) us.

[51.] However, when our consciousness (a certain young man) is centered in Spirit and has a divinely-inspired orientation (followed Him), our spiritually energetic inner life becomes apparent (they caught hold of him) through our glowing appearance (linen cloth). [52.] But our outer appearance (linen cloth) is only symbolic of our inner spiritual nature which is not confined to the limitations of human form (ran off naked).

Spiritual Limbo
Spirited Away

[53.] When we betray the higher aspects of our spiritual nature, we tend to rely on an intellectual understanding (high priest) and a worldly interpretation (chief priests, elders and scribes) of our spiritual experiences. ⁵⁴·Even though we have developed powers far beyond the less spiritually attuned person, our faith (our Peter quality) in our ability to divinely order our continued spiritual growth may falter in the presence of rigid religious views (guards) which prompt us to reconsider (warm ourselves by the fire) our hesitance to apply the truths we know. ⁵⁵·We find ourselves in a stage of growth that can be likened to a sort of spiritual limbo where our material nature, steeped in its endless sense attachments, sees opportunities to kill spiritual aspirations. ⁵⁶·However, our materially-minded ego is unable to comprehend the extent of our spiritual unfoldment. And so it relies on its chief conspirators—old, established religious assumptions (false testimonies) ⁵⁷·as fabricated foundations (standing up) to justify (give false testimony) its material focus. ⁵⁸·We allow these purely sense-bleached aspects of our psyche to tempt us to challenge the very notion of our being able to divinely order our experience (represented by three days—mind, idea, and expression). ⁵⁹·Although our ego challenges the Divine Order process, it has no comprehension of how it works.

⁶⁰·When faced with the task of sorting out higher consciousness nuances, the unenlightened ego remains clueless. ⁶¹·Unfortunately, if we remain a product of our materially-focused personality, which is controlled by an unaware ego, we may refuse to slow down long enough to hear the still small voice. Instead, our sense-corrupted ego wants material proof of our spiritual divinity. ⁶²·Rest assured, when we remain steadfast in our desire to rise completely above the illusion of separation, the need for religious dogma, and a desire for material attachments, we will be at a place in our spiritual growth (seated at the right hand) in which our con-

sciousness of Truth (coming with the clouds of heaven) is attuned with the consciousness of the Christ as us. [63.] When we reach that level of adeptship, the recalcitrant ego's lack of understanding (torn garments) is so pronounced that it retreats into the safe harbor of its illusions (no need for witnesses). [64.] Seeking to dampen our awareness of being able to actualize our Christ potential, the ego prompts us to kill any and all possible growth of our Christ potential. [65.] So, it attacks our notion of the Christ of us the only way it knows. It arrogantly, and with as much malice as it can muster, shows its resentment (spittle) of higher truths it considers as threats to its corporal influence by blurring (blindfolding) the lines between Truth and error. Confusing power with force, the ego depends on logical, material constructs (guards) to assert its rulership.

Denying Our Divinity

[66.] As we near the cusp of our Christship, our faith (our Peter faculty) will be put to the test, so we must be ready to withstand the alienation (the courtyard below) of worldly inclinations. However, there is that unquickened intuitive quality within us (servant girl) [67.] that, despite its dogmatic origin, reminds us of our self-avowed oneness with Spirit. [68.] Doubting our ability to remain Christed, we may even deny our connection to Spirit to compensate for belief in our unworthiness. As soon as this level of doubt hits our consciousness, there is that Christed quality within us that readily sounds an internal spiritual alarm (cock crows) and urges us to purge any and all anti-Christed thoughts out of our consciousness. [69.] In spite of what seems to be the innocent questioning of our unquickened intuition (servant-girl), [70.] denying our connection to Spirit is not a

Christed response. Such progressive denial begins to affect a growing number of areas in our psyche, including the recesses of our subconscious (Galilee). [71.] If we should get to the point where we adamantly deny our connection to Spirit because we feel pressured by the slings and arrows of outer appearances, [72.] we will experience an incredibly disconcerting inner alarm (cock crows a second time) which signals a spiritual disconnect between faith in our divinity and hope for our divine status. If our faith degenerates to that point we will have essentially compromised the spiritual growth of our body, mind, and soul (three denials).

Chapter Fifteen

Our Carnal Mind Seeks Spiritual Answers to Material Questions

[1.] When we give in to our sense nature, our thoughts are centered on the pleasures of this world and we usually are in no mood to entertain thoughts about the spiritual side of life. So we purposefully censor our connection with Spirit and allow our carnal will (our Pilate faculty) to define who we are. [2.] Because of our choosing to operate out of a Pilate perspective, we have an uneasiness about us, generated from a paranoid ego that is faced with the prospect of it being neutralized by our quest for Christhood. So it (the worldly ego) seeks to protect itself and its encrusted religious dogmatism by assuring itself that the object of our spiritual aspirations should not be to dethrone it from its sterile religious perch. The Christ of us knows the unenlightened ego is incapable of gaining the clarity it needs, and merely wants confirmation of its rulership over the lower, more sense-oriented aspects of our human beingness. Spirit responds to this vacillation between Truth and error by encouraging our search for wholeness without giving us the impression It will unfold our wholeness for us. 3. Unfortunately, our error consciousness is clueless of this possibility and predictably misses the point. 4. Our carnal mind (our Pilate faculty), driven by its sense appetites, hears the clamor (charges brought against the Christ) of our sense thoughts and uses its worldly biases to mock our Christed perspective. 5. But the Christ of us sees only (makes no reply) the higher aspects of our beingness.

Messiahing or Rebelling

6. As we consider the full implications of transcending our error consciousness 7. we will find it necessary to release any rebelliousness or opposition we feel about our worthiness and competence to become one with Spirit (our Barabbas qualities). 8. That whole introspective process can be very confusing. 9. So, we have a decision to make. Do we hold on to our rebelliousness (our Barabbas nature) or do we continue our Messiahing toward our Christhood? 10. We are faced with this dilemma any time we attempt to appease a willful ego which is extremely jealous of our spiritual nature, which it fears is gaining entirely too much influence over us. 11. And yet, if we aren't careful, we will succumb to our rebelliousness and postpone our Christhood. If we are truly one with Spirit, we will release our opposition (Barabbas instinct) in order to consummate our Christhood. 12. Once we make the Christ decision, our mortal mind (Pilate) is powerless to withhold our I-am-ness (King of the Jews) which enlivens our consciousness and turns our rebelliousness into spiritual

aspiration. [13.] Our immediate response is to deny our error-prone human limitations and unite in consciousness with our Christ Self. [14.] Our carnal mind (Pilate) is out of the picture because it fails to comprehend the spiritual connection between its demise as ruler of our mortal personality and our metamorphosis into our Christed Individuality. [15.] This phase of our attunement is an extremely difficult phase because our mortal personality (Pilate), sensing that a complete release of its rebelliousness (our Barabbas faculty) is necessary, will nevertheless intensify its resistance to a spiritual direction which it believes threatens its very existence. It reacts by launching a barrage (flogs our Jesus quality) of deeply-rooted beliefs in the supremacy of the material over the spiritual.

Making a Mockery Out of Ourselves

[16.] As our resistance intensifies, we try to rationalize what is happening to us from a purely intellectual perspective (the governor's headquarters). [17.] We attempt to mock the Truth from a materialistic perspective (clothing him in purple) to show that there is no real kingdom for Spirit to rule. Finding it difficult to separate ourselves from our mortal appetites, we may twist the Truth (crown of thorns) by formulating our own version of it to perpetuate our illusions. [18.] We may even flout our ignorance of the Truth by denying our innate I-Am-ness (shouting "Hail, King of the Jews"). [19.] If our human personality is adamant in its refusal to become receptive to our higher spiritual essence we may blatantly show our disrespect for our divine nature (spit on our Christ potential). We may attack the very notion of our

Christhood (striking the head) by preferring to remain stuck (kneel down in homage) in sense consciousness. [20.] Unable to clothe Truth in material language (put His own clothes on Him), the confused intellect is reminded once again that the Truth is greater than the mortal mind can comprehend. The mortal mind has entered unfamiliar spiritual territory and has naturally become affected by the power of Spirit. This phase of our unfoldment is characterized by the frightened ego's attempts to save itself from the annihilation it suspects it is facing. Its swan song takes us closer to uniting our whole personality with the Christ of us (led Him away to be crucified).

Crossing Out Error and Duality

[21.] If we dutifully walk the principled path, encrusted religious thoughts and erroneous material beliefs (Simon of Cyrene) which have burdened us for so long will be overcome. [22.] By overcoming any and all sense limitations we allow Spirit Its eternal ascendancy and we enter that phase of our spiritual unfoldment in which we transcend carnal consciousness (Golgotha) and move into Christ Consciousness. [23.] We have quite literally chosen the eternal over imperfection (wine mixed with gall and myrrh). [24.] When we have allowed the Spirit as us to cross out all error (we are crucified), we can attain immortality by renouncing all personal ties which would in any way compromise our absolute and complete harmonization with our Christ Self. We have the wherewithal to completely discern the difference (divided clothing) between our I-Am-ness and the transformed sense-body which housed our Christhood for so long. [25.] At every level of our being, the trinity of trinities (number nine), we have crossed out error (are crucified), [26.] and the distinction between the human personality and the Christ Personality gives way to a consciousness of oneness and wholeness. [27.] Our belief in duality (two bandits) is wiped out of our consciousness. [28.] But this whole process depends on our resolve to take a look at our human limitations (be counted among the lawless) and then choose our Christship over sense-ship. [29.] Our error consciousness becomes a thing of the past. We recognize the Truth about the outpicturing of Divine Order and realize the immense implications of honoring our I-Am-ness. [30.] The invitation to refrain from crossing error out of our consciousness (come down from the cross) is no longer part of our makeup. [31.] In our old Pharisaical state of consciousness we failed to understand this because we were living, moving, and having our being in a blind state of consciousness, one characterized by selfishness and religious glaucoma. [32.] These two negative qualities are always under the influence of outer appearances. In that ruptured state of consciousness, we worshipped the flesh and the things of the flesh. We made our residence in coma consciousness and refused to see our true connection with Spirit. That is why our belief in duality (good and evil) presents such a barrier to our spiritual unfoldment.

Gaining Immortality

[33.] As the crossing out error process penetrates our subconsciousness (darkness comes over the land) we divinely order (three in the afternoon) Truth over error. [34.] And when Divine Order is established (three o'clock), we can affirm confidently and joyfully, "My God, My God, it is for this purpose I have come!" [35.] The power of our words confirm our conscious connection with our

I-Am-ness (our Elijah essence). ³⁶· The bitterness (sour wine) caused by the illusion of our separation gives way to the sweetness of our oneness with Spirit and we fully anticipate our complete entrainment into our I-Am-ness (our Elijah essence). ³⁷· Because we are consciously and cellularly one with Spirit we are able to transcend all human limitations (breathe our last) and enjoy the immortality that was our birthright from the beginning. ³⁸· We are able to stand as a testament to all that it is possible for every one of us to see through the illusion of separation (the renting of the veil) which was ours to see from our conception. ³⁹· Our mortal will (centurian) becomes one with Divine Will and we celebrate our Christship.

⁴⁰· An important point to remember is that by honoring our intuitive intelligence and heightened receptivity to Truth (the women who followed the Christ) ⁴¹· we are able to concretize our ability to attune ourselves to Divine Ideas and transform those Ideas into materialized Substance (provide for Him). It is through this perfect receptivity (the two Marys and Salome) that we can divinely order our experiences. The nature of this receptivity is so powerful and quickened that the receptors of many of our spiritual faculties (other women) become even more sensitized to Spirit so that we can truly say we have become one with the peace (Jerusalem) which passes all misunderstanding.

The Gateway to Eternal Life

⁴²· From this heightened spiritual perspective we have a pronounced inner sense (the Day of Preparation for the Sabbath) ⁴³· of the deepening of our metamorphosis. It seems that our entire consciousness is filled with a potent mixture of God Essence so that our interior spiritual nature (our Joseph

of Arimathea quality) is humming expectantly for total and absolute enlightenment. [44.] It is at this bifurcation point in consciousness that our mortal mind (Pilate) tests our willfulness (centurian) to see if there is any possibility that we might still be clinging to duality and the built-in sense of separation it begets. [45.] At this point in our spiritual transformation, it becomes clear that we are not our physical bodies, and that what was once our mortal body has now become a vehicle for enlightment. [46.] In this increasingly vivified state of spiritual unfoldment we can prepare to enter the exalted gateway in consciousness (Arimathea's unused tomb) which leads to life eternal. This mystic thoroughfare is protected by our Indwelling Christ (the stone rolled across entrance to tomb). [47.] Our love and devotion (both Marys) for the Truth will keep us grounded in the Divine Connection.

Chapter Sixteen

The Restorative Power of the Resurrection Experience

[1.] When we have reached the perfect stage of our spiritual unfoldment, which is complete rest (the Sabbath) from error consciousness, a new plane of transcendental expression is imminent. Our highest essences of receptivity, selfless love in service to others, a superior intuition (the two Marys), and spiritual wholeness (Salome) [2.] prepare us to enter the gateway (tomb) which leads to an extraordinarily high level of consciousness (early in the day). [3.] Even though we are attuned to this high level of spiritual unfoldment, we may still stumble across a repressed thought or two of separation (who will roll away the stone?) as we move toward the gateway (tomb) leading to Christ Consciousness. [4.] However, all we have to do is keep our thoughts Christed (look up), and any sense of duality and separation will disappear (the stone is rolled back). ⁵·In this state of illumination, our intellect (the young man) has reached its highest state of spiritual development (dressed in a white robe) by becoming one with our spiritualized intuition (sitting on the right side), which tends to disorient us (alarm us) for a time since we have not been used to the complete and absolute harmonization of our two brain hemispheres. ⁶·The wisdom of our purified heart and our electrified intuitive intelligence (the three women) realize that we have just evolved from our Christ potential (our Jesus of Nazareth quality) which has taken us beyond the mortal into the immortal (crucified us) and metamorphasized us into our Christhood (He has been raised). It occurs to us immediately that our Christhood has always been our destiny (the empty tomb). ⁷·Because of our absolute faith (our quickened Peter quality) in the process, the life currents in our subconsciousness (Galilee) will feel the effects of our Christedness and be likewise transformed. ⁸·As these super-spiritualized qualities (the three women) begin their transformative descents into our subconscious depths, we are amazed at our exalted spiritual status on the one hand and unsure of the total implications of our transformation on the other.

The Magdalene Effect

⁹·One of the first things we notice in our newly-formed Christed awareness is that our soul consciousness (Mary Magdalene), characterized by its fundamentally attenuated feeling nature (seven demons), has completely metamorphasized into its higher spiritual essence in every respect. ¹⁰·It is this psychical sensitivity which

is able to comprehend our Christship and integrate the Christed us into our new beingness. [11.] It is quite common during the inaugural moments of our newly-acquired Christhood that our developing consciousness will need a few moments to acclimate itself to its Christship.

When Potential Becomes Actualized

[12.] It is not an exaggeration to say that our newly-acquired Christship requires a huge leap in consciousness and will depend on our heightened receptivity and unequivocal sense of wholeness (he appears to two of them) to help us appreciate our transformation. [13.] We will need time, though, to understand our incredible unfoldment.

Commissioning Our Consciousness for Christhood

[14.] Even though our spiritual powers (eleven disciples) are highly developed and basically attuned (sitting together at the table), we must still seek to develop them further. [15.] We must develop our newly transformed body, mind, and spirit by affirming that we have broken the bonds of duality and separation and have become Christs (the good news). [16.] When we keep our thoughts pure and Christed (a baptismal experience) we will keep our consciousness cleansed (saved) from error thoughts. If we neglect to stay Christed in our thinking, we will lose spiritual tone (condemn ourselves) and slow, or even interrupt, our spiritual progress. [17.] We will know when we have arrived, so to speak, because we will live, move, and have our being from our Christ Consciousness (in the name of) so that we will have no difficulty erasing (casting out) any error thoughts (demons) which seek to intrude into our consciousness. We will easily be able to understand higher levels of Truth (speak in tongues) so that we can offer new perspectives and insights, which lead to higher degrees of health and wholeness. [18.] We will be able to recognize (pick up) the temptations of sense consciousness (snakes) and elevate sense thoughts to their higher spiritual counterparts. We will gain mastery (drink) over any falsehood (deadly thing) so that it will not block our spiritual growth; and we will effortlessly use our spiritual powers for the benefit of humankind.

Ascended Mastery

[19.] And so when our Christ potential (our individualized Jesus quality) is actualized (spoken), our entire consciousness is bathed in Truth (heaven) and we will have completed our unfoldment as a Christ (sit at the right hand) in the realm of Absolute Good (God). [20.] Once we reach that level of Christ Consciousness, our Christhood Itself is the fulfillment of our absolute and individualized Divinity (the good news which has been constantly communicated to us ever since we incarnated as human beings).

*B*il Holton, Ph.D. currently shares spiritual leadership responsibilities with his wife, Cher, in the growing Unity Spiritual Life Center they co-minister in Durham, North Carolina. He is a Licensed Unity Teacher, and has been affiliated with the Unity spiritual education movement for thirty years. As a student of metaphysics for over twenty years, Dr. Holton believes Biblical scripture has a deeper spiritual meaning, which enriches the literal text and elevates it beyond its dogmatic and parochial limitations.

His spiritual mission is to lead, guide, and inspire people all over the world to live faithfully, lovingly, and wisely at the speed of their Christ Consciousness. While he has authored and co-authored over twenty books with Cher, Bil believes his metaphysical translations of the Gospels are his most fulfilling works to date.

On a personal note, the Holtons like to push the envelope and maintain their zest for life by taking what they call "Indiana Jones Adventures," such as white-water rafting, sky diving, and fire walking. American-style ballroom dancing is also in their DNA. Although they have retired their competitive dance shoes, Bil and Cher love to perform ballroom showcases and exhibitions. Their two sons, beautiful daughters-in-law, and two incredible grandchildren, all live nearby. Their visits are always joyful.

To order copies of *The Gospel of Matthew, New Metaphysical Version* or *The Gospel of Mark, New Metaphysical Version;* place orders for *The New Metaphysical Versions of Luke and John;* and request information about scheduling Dr. Bil Holton for speaking engagements, visit his website at http://www.metaphysicalbible.net or call his office at 877.819.7489.

You may contribute to the New Metaphysical Version Project, which supports Dr. Holton's work, by visiting the official website, http://www.metaphysicalbible.net or by contacting Dr. Holton at his toll-free office number, 877.819.7489.